JACQUES
VILLENEUVE

As part of our ongoing market research, we are always pleased to receive comments about our books, suggestions for new titles, or requests for catalogues. Please write to: The Editorial Director, Patrick Stephens Limited, Sparkford, Nr Yeovil, Somerset BA22 7JJ.

JACQUES
VILLENEUVE

IN HIS OWN RIGHT

Christopher Hilton

Patrick Stephens Limited

First published in 1996

British Library Cataloguing-in-Publication Data:
A catalogue record for this book is
available from the British Library

ISBN: 1 85260 557 X

Library of Congress catalog card no. 95 82340

Patrick Stephens Limited is an imprint of Haynes Publishing,
Sparkford, Nr Yeovil, Somerset BA22 7JJ.

Designed and typeset by G&M, Raunds, Northamptonshire
Printed in Britain by Butler & Tanner Ltd, London and Frome

Contents

Acknowledgements

SINCERE THANKS TO Gianni Berti of the Commissione Sportiva Automobilistica Italiana, Rome; Ann Bradshaw of Williams Grand Prix Engineering; Peter Dick; Amy Riley and Bob Walters, Public Relations, Indianapolis Motor Speedway; Julian Thomas; Christiano Chiavegato of *La Stampa*, Turin; Patrick Tambay; Hiroshi Fushida of TOM's Toyota; Richard Spenard; Vince Laughran of the Jim Russell Driving School, Mont Tremblant, Canada; Pete Spence of Cosinc, California; Gilles Bourcier of *La Presse*, Montreal; *Autosport*'s Nigel Roebuck, Marcus Pye, Laurence Foster and especially Gordon Kirby for his IndyCar race reports and help to unravel technical factors; Mauro Martini; Dr Sue Holder of the Kennedy Galton Centre, Northwick Hospital, London; Rickard Rydell; Ingmar Hesslefors of Volvo Car Corporation; David Phillips of *Motoring News*; Claude Bourbonnais; Tony Cicale; L'Automobil Club d'Andorra; David Hatter's excellent feature in *Formula 2000*, Montreal; Daniel L. du Plessis, Canapress, Montreal; Pierre and Yula de Meyer of the Beau Soleil International Alpine College, Villars; Luigi and Massimo Buratti; Angelo Rosin and Simone Battistella of the PreMa Power Team; Barry Green of Team Green; Monica Meroni for organising interviews; Giovanna Farrell-Vinay for translation.

I am particularly indebted to Marco Ragazzoni of *Autosprint* for help above and beyond the call of duty. I've used the magazine's reportage extensively. I've drawn on *Gilles Villeneuve: The Life of the Legendary Racing Driver* by Gerald Donaldson (MRP) and leant heavily on the British magazines *Autosport* and *Motoring News*. Thanks respectively to Simon Taylor, Chairman, Haymarket Publications, and Simon Arron, Editor, for permission to quote. The Indianapolis 500 Daily Trackside Report for 1994 was invaluable, as was the Marlboro Grand Prix Guide.

Straight from the grid

THE COMPARISON WAS, as it was always going to be, too direct, too *umbilical* to resist.

One July afternoon in 1977 a 27-year-old from Quebec, born in a town with a rolling lilt of a name — Saint-Jean-sur-Richelieu — came to a test session at Silverstone and eased himself into a Formula 1 car for the first time. He pressed it along the pit lane, accelerated and moved out onto a completely unfamiliar racing circuit. The corners rearing at him bore very English names which did not lilt — Becketts, Chapel, Stowe, Club, Abbey — and each made particular demands on a man and his machine, as he would discover.

One August afternoon in 1995 a 24-year-old from Quebec, also born in Saint-Jean-sur-Richelieu, came to a test session at Silverstone and eased himself into a Formula 1 car for the first time. He pressed it along the pit lane, accelerated and moved out onto a completely unfamiliar racing circuit. The corners rearing at him bore the same names — Becketts, Chapel, Stowe, Club, Abbey — but their contours had been radically altered across the years in between. Each still made their particular demands on man and machine, as he would discover. But they were different.

In a sharp sense that word — different — is the theme of this book and it will recur throughout. Comparisons between the two men were inevitable, and invalid.

Gilles Villeneuve arrived at Silverstone to force his way into Formula 1 and, wielding a McLaren, attacked the circuit. He hadn't much time. He was to make his Grand Prix debut that week. In order to find the limits of this car as quickly as possible he repeatedly drove beyond its limits. Normally drivers approach this from the other direction by feeling towards the limits. He spun repeatedly, convulsively, dangerously. (In Gerald Donaldson's book, the estimate is 20 times.) He didn't mind. The European mythology of Villeneuve — another word which will interweave as a theme — began then. It has not gone away and reached full across the years to August 1995.

Jacques Villeneuve, the son of Gilles, was at Silverstone to look, learn and ponder Formula 1. Wielding a Williams, he did not attack the circuit. The Williams team were struck by how calm he seemed, how clinical, how *cool*. Within these self-imposed restraints, however, he was proving he was fast too. In three days of testing he spun only once, at Becketts. In 1977 his father had spun there also and surely more than once . . .

Soon enough, Jacques committed himself to Williams and Formula 1 for 1996. He'd just become the youngest IndyCar Champion for more than four decades. In Formula 1 he would have to bear the expectations of The Name bequeathed to him, have to accept other people for ever gazing at him as *the son*. In one way this was easy enough because it had trailed him all his life and, anyway, he was proud of his father's memory and achievements. But he insisted he was his own man and doing this strictly on merit. He said this quietly, and deliberately, and firmly, not least because it was true. You can travel so far on paternal reputation and then, very suddenly, it works against you. Ask Damon Hill, Villeneuve's partner in 1996.

Perhaps in a sense Jacques Villeneuve had endured The Name. Certainly in the early days of his career it provoked enormous interest long before he could justify it. That brought inevitable consequences and comparisons because The Name carried no ordinary associations.

If Gilles Villeneuve had been just another driver, albeit a famous one, that wouldn't have been the same thing. But the enduring affection for Gilles Villeneuve is deeper than any cursory examination of his career might suggest (67 Grands Prix, two pole positions, six victories). He was an unspoilt human being — which touched all who knew him — and a real racer. Of the 67 Grands Prix, all but one were in Ferraris of various states of undriveability. From this he constructed precious moments of wheel-to-wheel combat (and closer), hurling the cars until they were sideways and keeping the accelerator hard down. Once in a stinking wet qualifying session at Watkins Glen, New York State, he was fastest by *11 seconds*; and more of the same until his death at Zolder, Belgium, in 1982, when, going for pole, he struck another car. A yard either way might have been different, but that's the yard motor racing doesn't always allow you.

When death takes someone heroic in their prime — someone aged only 32 — it deepens mourning and defines mythology. I think we must accept that premise, although there is another dimension to consider. Italy adores Ferrari, Ferrari adores racers, Italy adores racers, and virtually everyone adored Gilles Villeneuve. Forged together these factors became an emotion so powerful it was not temporal.

For the son to embark on the same route is either a brave decision or a dubious one. The route is strewn with obstacles, not least the level of expectation, the people who gaze, and the comparison. Jacques speaks of the swell of interest when he started racing at 17, of how it forced him to "mature quickly" or be overwhelmed; but the son had advantages. A North American, he'd grown up in Europe and was comfortably cross-cultural. (His immediate predecessor from IndyCars to Formula 1, Michael Andretti, was consumed by the differences and went home.) An account of a further test session, at Monza — he'd won the IndyCar championship the week before — says this: "Villeneuve impressed the large press following by conducting a press conference in English, Italian and French."

Jacques had also grown up in motor racing because, from the early days, Gilles had taken the family around with him from circuit to circuit in a camper. A life within racing is arguably a very abnormal life unless you have travelled within it since the age of five, as he had.

In the matter of inheritance, Jacques has said: "Some things are

New world. Villeneuve tests the Williams Formula 1 car (ICN U.K. Bureau).

retained from your parents. I hopefully retained the good things." Certainly there is a strong physical likeness between father and son. However, the fact that a man was a great racing driver does not guarantee that his progeny will be one also, any more than a great painter will spawn a great painter or a great statesman (if you can find one) will bestow another such upon us. None of this prevents the son emulating the father but at some point he must do it *as if his father hadn't been who he was*. There is conclusive evidence to suggest that, once the career was properly launched, Jacques Villeneuve did exactly that. His route and his manner of travelling the route — racing schools in Canada, the perils of Formula 3 in Italy, the relative sanctuary of Japan, the steps to IndyCar, the IndyCar triumph — strongly argue that he was his own man and, after a difficult start, he was doing this on merit. A noted Italian journalist, Christiano Chiavegato, interviewed him in 1988 and he said: "I am Jacques Villeneuve, not Gilles Villeneuve." Seven years later Chiavegato listened as he accepted an award in Italy and he said: "I am Jacques Villeneuve, not Gilles Villeneuve." He still felt he had to say it.

When he pressed the Williams car out of the pit lane and accelerated at Silverstone in August 1995 the interest quickly shifted from who he was to what he could make the car do. And he could make it do competitive times, repeatedly, sensibly, smoothly. In November, at yet more testing, in Estoril, he explained that the team were staying an extra day in the hope that it would rain. He wanted to explore the car in the wet, learn what he could prudently make it do in such conditions.

We were at a far remove from the intuitive bravura of Gilles. We were at the beginning, in Formula 1 terms, of something else altogether.

As that beginning moved closer — mid February, with the first race in Australia only three weeks away — Villeneuve and Hill took time out from further testing at the favoured haunt, Estoril, to give a global satellite press conference from the pits. Villeneuve was at ease, affable, and entirely realistic.

"It is a huge challenge," he said of Formula 1. "This is the top in racing. The IndyCar Championship is a good championship, but Formula 1 is *the* racing series. Of course, being with the top team, and having all the preparation we have had so far, *and* coming here after winning in the States, there won't be any excuses."

Testing, he said, was the only way to prepare. "But you can't replace the racing with testing. What you get in the racing is tough decisions, fighting with other drivers (in the competitive sense), strategy, starts, pressure, things you can't touch when you're testing. You could do a million miles and you still wouldn't have those few things."

What did he have? The world would find out, very soon now.

• CHAPTER ONE •

The inheritance

THE MOST RECENT branches of the Villeneuve family tree are entirely relevant today. Gilles Villeneuve was born on 18 January 1950 and began racing competitively in 1973. He had a brother, Jacques, born on 4 November 1953. Gilles married Joann Barthe on 17 October 1970. She was pregnant. The child, named Jacques after Gilles' brother, was born on 9 April 1971. A daughter, Melanie, was born on 26 July 1973.

Gilles Villeneuve, unaffected by adulation and fame, made many friends and many more admirers. The bond between the urbane Frenchman Patrick Tambay and the young French-Canadian began in 1976. "The first time I met him was in Formula Atlantic at Trois Rivieres [a 2.10 mile circuit by the St. Laurence river between Quebec and Montreal]," Tambay says.

"A year later we raced against one another in Canada in Can-Am, and when I was over there I stayed with him. At the time he was driving for Wolf [Walter Wolf, Austrian born Canadian who'd made a vast fortune in oil and was actively involved in racing]. However in 1977 Gilles had a contract to do the British Grand Prix with McLaren, his first Grand Prix, and I had one with the Ensign team — my first Grand Prix as well.

"When Gilles came to Europe in 1977 he stayed with us at our

The Villeneuves, January 1979. From left to right: Gilles, Gilles' mother Georgette, Melanie, Jacques (Yves Beauchamp/Canapress).

house in Villars in Switzerland. We were very good friends. He brought Jacques and Melanie so I met Jacques when he was around six. He destroyed my stereo! He played with it and burnt the whole thing. I don't know what happened or how he did it (chuckle) . . ."

For that British Grand Prix, on 16 July, Villeneuve qualified on the fifth row and Tambay the eighth. Villeneuve ran seventh until the temperature gauge flicked into the red. He pitted but it seemed the gauge was misbehaving so he went out again two laps down and finished eleventh. Tambay's electrics failed on lap four.

"After two or three races Mauro Forghieri of Ferrari came to me," Tambay says. "We had a meeting and he made me an offer for 1978. At the same time Teddy Mayer and John Hogan came to me with a McLaren offer. I signed for McLaren. I told Gilles that Ferrari had been on to me and pointed out that although McLaren had an option on him they probably wouldn't be picking it up. I told him to phone Ferrari to see if they'd be interested — they wanted a young number 2 guy to Carlos Reutemann for 1978. Ferrari, incidentally, were changing to Michelin tyres which was one of the reasons I didn't join them. I thought they wouldn't be competitive, which they were not."

And so it happened: Enzo Ferrari signed Villeneuve and would run three cars at the 1977 Canadian Grand Prix, for him, Reutemann and Niki Lauda; but Lauda suddenly walked away from the team before the race and there were only two. Villeneuve never drove for anyone else. In 1978 he brought the family to settle in Europe. "They stayed two months," Tambay says, "and we helped them with finding a house."

Tambay, who had a villa in the South of France, recommended they find somewhere in the area and they did, in the hills behind Cannes. It enabled the children to continue speaking French. In his study of Villeneuve, Donaldson quotes Joann as saying: "It was difficult for the kids because we were kind of isolated up there and they had to find their way around a new school. They adapted quickly and soon made friends but there was quite a culture shock at first for all of us."

The little lad grew into this. Jacques Villeneuve, September 1995, at Vancouver (Ray Giguere/Canapress).

In time the family moved to Monaco. Jacques would remember that. "A question that is very common is what I remember of my father, what makes me similar to him and if I want to do what he did," he wrote in the late 1980s in *Autosprint*. "People try to make me identify with my father at all costs but nobody really knows who Gilles Villeneuve was when he was with the family. This side of my father is still unknown because he was very jealous of his privacy and, believe me, it was not the attitude of a snob — he was sure people couldn't understand him even if they tried. I'll give you an example: the Monte Carlo villa.

"Some newspapers said that, with his success in Formula 1, he had become very bourgeois and bought a villa with a swimming pool because he couldn't be happy with a simple apartment. Do you want to know the true reason why my father bought this villa? He loved to work on cars enormously, he liked working on them with his hands and the villa was the only solution which allowed him to transform a garage into a fully equipped workshop.

"My mother tells me that, when they decided to buy, for him the most important thing was the garage, which had to be very big. To the great disappointment of my mother, the biggest and most beautiful houses were considered inadequate because their garages weren't what he wanted. The garage was his world. Often he didn't come to table for lunch and it was not unusual that, in the middle of the night and his hands covered in oil, he'd decide to go round Monte Carlo to try the latest modification he'd made to a car.

"His love for cars found expression not only when he was driving at circuits but in everything mechanical. We mustn't forget that he reached the point of going to all the Grands Prix in a camper in order to be constantly close to the Ferrari mechanics. This is the side of my father that is most fascinating to me."

The camper is part of the mythology. Nigel Roebuck remembers one evening at a Grand Prix when Gilles and Joann were eating at a table outside it and Gilles asked where little Jacques was. Roebuck, who'd walked via the pits, reported that little Jacques was playing

Right *The saddest time. Joann, Melanie and Jacques coming down the steps of a Canadian Air Force plane in Montreal two days after the death of Gilles* (Ron Poling/Canapress).

16

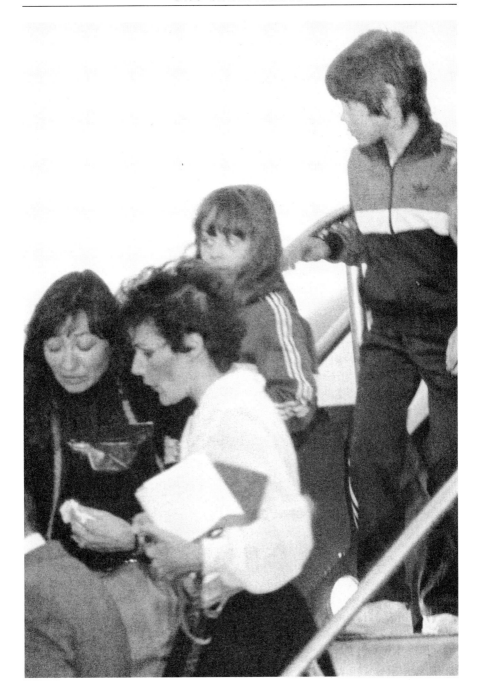

around with the mechanics. "That's OK then," Villeneuve said, as if this was the most normal thing in the world. In time Gilles would cover laps of Ferrari's test track at Fiorano in a road-going Ferrari, Jacques on his lap controlling the steering wheel while Gilles worked the pedals.

It broaches a central consideration. I'm indebted to Dr Sue Holder, a clinical geneticist, for her thoughts.

Can a racing driver inherit his abilities from a father who was a racing driver?

"The question is actually to do with the difference between environment and genetics in this situation. We inherit certain genes for characteristics like tallness, body shape, face — our features, certainly — but I'm talking about the sort of things that probably aren't due to just one gene but many, many genes.

"Intelligence certainly comes into that and other factors like dexterity. The question is how much does the environment that a chap is brought up in contribute to what he then chooses to do in his career? That's impossible to answer. Although he may well have inherited characteristics like being very quick in terms of his hands — in dealing with the controls or whatever — he wouldn't have inherited a desire to be a racing driver because that is almost certainly environmental; but some of the characteristics he has inherited may well make him a better racing driver. Those could just as easily be in a concert pianist whose father was a concert pianist, and he'll use those same beneficial characteristics to become a concert pianist. That's an environment he's familiar with, aware of and exposed to."

Could it include good eyesight, good reflexes?

"Good eyesight, yes, good reflexes — fast reflexes in terms of driving skill — yes, and dexterity."

Determination?

"Determination is difficult, isn't it, a bit nebulous? Our personalities are often very similar to our parents and I'd think that was a personality trait. It's partially inherited but it's also a lot to do with

Right *The funeral of Gilles, L'Eglise Ste-Genevieve-de-Berthier, Berthierville, Quebec, 12 May 1982. The man on the left, turned away from the camera, is Jody Scheckter, friend and former team-mate* (Bill Grimshaw/Canapress).

the environment and that's what you can't separate for an issue like this."

The son is extremely clinical whereas the father was known to be, let's say, flamboyant.

"Well, that may be just a difference in upbringing. Perhaps 15, 20 or 30 years ago you had to be a bit reckless on the track, whereas these days it's a different generation. Everything's computerised and controlled. Before, they just used to climb into their cars and go, didn't they?"

We're talking about a very safety-conscious era now.

"Again, it makes it difficult to interpret in terms of genetic constitution."

In sum, the fact that your father was a high-level driver does not automatically make you one, but what you receive from him, allied to growing up within the racing atmosphere, does seem to give you a better-than-average chance.

From 1977 Gilles Villeneuve became a legend. After his death on 8 May 1982 in final qualifying for the Belgian Grand Prix, he became the mythology too. Jacques was just past his 11th birthday.

"We were very, very good friends with Joann," Tambay says, "and when Gilles passed away she was taking it hard. I was living at Villars and we suggested to her that she put the kids into a boarding college near us. She couldn't handle them, they were on their own and she wasn't sleeping much — the kind of problems that you can have — and we suggested a college in Villars. We'd be close to them for any needs they may have and from a short distance we could overlook their well-being. We were also friends with the people at the college. I got to know Jacques well at 11, 12, 13 when we went ski-ing together and so on, and a few times he came to me for advice on sporting matters."

Did he want to be a driver?

"Well, he never said so — or at least never said he wanted to badly — but everything he did was actually going in that direction. He's always been very quiet and very poised and probably very determined about it, but he wasn't saying every day it was what he wanted; or showing off, you know, *I'm going to be a racing driver*. He was not, and

Right *12 May 1982* (Bill Grimshaw/Canapress).

is not, like his father at all. He is very calm. He calculates a lot. He's not as outspoken and as generous — in terms of being outgoing — as Gilles was.

"I think Jacques is a calculator. Because of his control he can probably achieve a lot more than Gilles did if he has some of the talent that Gilles had — and it's probably the case — plus the ability to be strategic in his approach to racing which he seems to have. He could be a combination of Gilles' speed and Alain Prost's thinking and that could be a hell of a combination."

One report says that, after the death of Gilles, Joann knew "she couldn't fill the void that he had left and tried with all her strength

Right *The happier times. August 1983 and Jacques has a look at the presentation made to Joann when Gilles was inducted into the Canadian Sports Hall of Fame* (Hans Deryk/Canapress).

Below *The Villeneuves at the induction ceremony. Grandparents Seville and Georgette are behind* (Hans Deryk/Canapress).

to prevent the children seeing how big the void was. From time to time, understandably, she was indulgent regarding discipline and school. Melanie, who seemed to have been hit the hardest at the beginning, reacted with energy and got involved in school work, obtaining good results. Jacques, instead, became more and more demotivated. He studied a minimum and sometimes not even that. She put both of them into college. If they had stayed at the family home it would have been very difficult."

To reach the Beau Soleil International Alpine College you must leave the autoroute which flows round Lake Leman and climb a tortuous little road into the mountains. As you pass through slumbering villages, the eaves of heavy wooden buildings overhang the road and many houses have sheds heaped with logs for the winter. This is heartland Switzerland.

Villars, at 1300 metres above sea level, is heartland Switzerland, too, and the official guide captures it nicely. "Our wish is to provide, amidst the splendours of our scenery, the joys offered by all forms of ski-ing and of other sports and to combine these pleasures with modern comfort, excellent cooking and a variety of entertainment." From the college, a solid building which looks like a college (a touch sombre and dignified), the splendour is all around: an immortal, immense panorama of Alpine peaks.

The college is bi-lingual and has a family atmosphere fostered by Pierre and Yula de Meyer, who run it. There are between 120 and 130 boarders who can follow either the French or American/British educational systems.

Yula remembers that "Jacques was 12 or 13 when he came. He seemed very young, small, but a boy without too many problems. He was lively, alert, he had a lot of interests and he was extremely *sportif*. In ski-ing he excelled and won races. He accepted the risks but he studied those risks: he calculated, he never jumped without knowing what lay ahead. He wasn't a boy who just went BOOOM. Kids tend to be a bit fou-fou (crazy). Not Jacques. He was a good downhiller and good at slalom — and in slalom (where, tight-tight-tight, you weave between 'gates') he almost always finished. He fell rarely. If he wanted to get to the end, he'd get to the end."

One of the advantages of Villars was that it allowed ski-ing every day in the season and, although ski racing is dangerous — 11 fatali-

Yula de Meyer in the reception area of the Beau Soleil International Alpine College at Villars (Author).

Pierre de Meyer, who still feels Jacques should have finished his exams! (Author).

ties worldwide between 1959 and January 1996 — the danger is not, perhaps, comparable to motor racing. Canada had a proper tradition in downhill, starting with the 'Crazy Canucks' in the mid-1970s led by Ken Read (who was also interested in Formula 1 and a regular spectator at the Canadian Grand Prix). Villeneuve might have tried to go in this direction and no doubt Joann would have been mightily relieved. Jacques remembers that "since I was very small I always loved sport: any discipline which involved action, like ski-ing and ice hockey. I devoted my time to school and ski-ing. I took part in races and won some of them. I was far from the world of cars, especially racing cars."

Mind you, Yula de Meyer says that "he had photographs of racing cars in his room, he was very into cars, but I must say all the boys of his age have a 'relationship' with racing cars!"

Interestingly, Beau Soleil had a games master and ski instructor called Craig Pollock, and that's where Villeneuve met him. Pollock would become a confidante and later his manager.

While Joann travelled to Villars each weekend to see Jacques and Melanie, Tambay, godfather of Jacques, decided to issue a challenge. He scanned Jacques' reports in 1983 and 1984 and said: "If you *want* to do it, you can become top of the class. If you succeed I'll give you a computer." Jacques succeeded and duly received a Commodore 64.

Yula de Meyer says "that was exactly Jacques. Every time, he could do whatever he wanted but if it wasn't necessary, if it wasn't vital, he'd say 'why tire myself out?' He was intelligent — no, very intelligent — with an excellent memory. He was *complete*. He could study as easily as he could amuse himself. A good pupil without working too much! I'd describe him as without complexes and without pretentions. In my opinion he was always going to succeed in whatever he chose because he'd know exactly where he wanted to go. In comparison to other boys of his age, he was mature."

Joann issued a challenge of her own. In the winter of 1984 Jacques said the words she wished she'd never hear. "Do you know that it is enough to be 12 to be able to compete in karts?"

No, she didn't.

"Well, just think. I've lost two years already!"

She doesn't remember what she replied but the subject returned. She did what Patrick had done: Jacques was weak in maths and if he improved "I'd allow him to drive a kart." At the end of the year Jacques obtained a mark of 15 "which is very good so I had to keep my promise."

In June 1985 the Villeneuves were on holiday in Canada and Paolo Moruzzi of SAGIS, the company which runs the circuit of Imola, was there, too, attending the Grand Prix as a guest of Gilles' parents. In conversation the subject of karting came up — Joann had her promise to keep — and Moruzzi said immediately that Jacques could have a go at Imola. Early one Friday in September, four months later, the Villeneuves — Joann, Jacques and Melanie — travelled from Monte Carlo to Imola in Joann's blue Ferrari 308. Reportedly Joann approached the whole thing like someone "having a tooth out."

I only wish they don't decide to become drivers — truly I don't want this

---

Moruzzi had contacted *Autosprint* and together they set up an arrangement with Luigi Buratti and his son Massimo of Bologna, the big town near Imola. Luigi, a small, jolly, engaging man, had been working on karts since 1959 and subsequently a variety of other vehicles too, including Formula 4 cars, a particularly Italian form of single-seaters designed to help kids get into racing. In the courtyard of their workshop, a place choked with machines and machinery, they loaded a basic 100cc kart, a 135cc competition kart and a Formula 4 car into their van and set off down the autostrada for Imola, intending to be there about 9 o'clock. It was a warm, sunny day.

They'd been "great fans of Gilles."

Jacques had evidently already done a bit of illicit driving around Monte Carlo with Joann in the passenger seat closely supervising. She recognised it as "a passion transmitted to Jacques by Gilles." Jacques had evidently done a bit of illicit driving in Canada, too. "My uncle Jacques let me try his Mustang on a stretch of safe and deserted road. I reached 200kph but my uncle was sitting beside me . . ."

Imola lay heavy with memories. During the Italian Grand Prix there in 1980 Gilles Villeneuve's right rear tyre exploded at 180mph at a corner called Tosa, sending the Ferrari into a wild spin. It hit a bank, destroying the car. He remained motionless in the cockpit — traditionally the most worrying sign. "One of my front wheels hit my helmet," he'd say, "and at that instant I lost my sight. I was completely blind. Although I could hear the other cars going by, very close, I decided not to try and get out while my sight was gone. After a few seconds it came back bit by bit."

During the San Marino Grand Prix there in 1982 Villeneuve felt that his team-mate Didier Pironi defied team orders and took advantage of him. A political dispute within Formula 1 meant that only 14 cars lined up on the grid. Pironi, the number 2 driver, passed Villeneuve for the lead, Villeneuve repassed and so it went on. Villeneuve assumed that with so few cars circulating Pironi had decided to put on a show for the crowd but would obediently move over near the end. Instead Pironi repassed with no time for Villeneuve to respond. Villeneuve, most trusting of men, felt openly betrayed and never spoke to Pironi again. Zolder was two weeks later.

That September day three years later Joann confessed that to watch a Grand Prix at Monaco had no effect on her but places like Imola and Montreal produced a "knot in the throat" because thoughts and memories came back so sharply. She was against the whole thing "but I have to keep the promise and, however unwillingly, I have accepted it. I only wish they don't decide to become drivers. Truly I don't want this."

Jacques looked small, almost slight, but recognisably a Villeneuve: the set of the face. Both he and Melanie were visibly relaxed at being in a racing environment which, of course, might have been an ordeal to others of such an age. The number of people present might have compounded that because a whole group were there to witness it, including Moruzzi, Roberto Nosetto (Ferrari team manager in Gilles' time) and Vittorio Zoboli, the Italian F4 champion.

One reporter noted that Jacques and Melanie "enacted the ritual of dressing up in overalls and putting helmets on without showing the slightest emotion — quite different to Joann who was very nervous in the pits." Jacques was momentarily puzzled by the presence of reporters and a photographer. Someone asked him "do you

Villars, heartland Switzerland (Author).

The view from the college (Author).

think it is possible for anyone with the name *Villeneuve* to drive at Imola without the press knowing?"

The Burattis unloaded the karts and the Formula 4 car (which *Autosprint*, in a deliciously ambiguous phrase, described as "just meant to be a choreographic presence"). The kart track, approximately 600 metres long, was entirely traditional, a snake of a thing marked out by rubber cones and old tyres. It contorted round the infield near the pits and embraced a section of the Grand Prix circuit itself. Jacques eased himself into the 100cc kart and — so this new legend goes — was already at the end of the straight before anyone could give him advice on how to drive it.

Ah, but we must be careful to resist the temptation to romance about this occasion, finding what people wanted it to be rather than what actually happened. The Burattis, you see, were both experienced teachers and, although they were "very happy to see this young Villeneuve, we are instructors so teaching was not a problem. We helped start the careers not only of Zoboli but also Gianni Morbidelli and Emanuele Pirro [who both reached F1]. However we took particular care that Jacques didn't have an accident. We felt a great responsibility and we were a bit worried about it." Overall, however, they felt "it was an honour."

The Burattis therefore explained about the kart and how to handle it and away Villeneuve went "slowly, very slowly, at the beginning and then we allowed him to go faster. He had a few spins but after that no problem."

The *Autosprint* reporter found the temptation too difficult. He quoted Luigi Buratti as saying: 'He certainly is a worthy son of the great Gilles. Without any experience whatsoever, he is able to go round almost at the limit and immediately he finds the ideal racing line.'" (When her turn came, Melanie was good, too, although slightly slower.)

Because Jacques had done so competently they gave him a 135cc kart but, the reporter wrote, "the difference in power didn't worry him. He was at ease straight away in the midst of the cones, which he passed by the millimetre." Jacques was described as "more violent" than Melanie whose driving was "more fluid and co-ordinated."

Then they had lunch (eating "like little wolves") and ribbed each other about their previous experience in karts. She said they'd already driven them at Montreux. "Silly girl," he interrupted, "they weren't karts, they were toys only good for children like you!" Joann insisted that it was a nice holiday and must remain so.

Autosprint reported that after lunch, "given the ease with which Jacques and Melanie were dealing with karts, somebody thought of the Formula 4 car. It didn't take much for Jacques to jump into the driving seat and have the pedals and seat adapted to him. He was smiling and totally at ease though this was his first contact with a single-seater." Zoboli explained about the five gears and warned to keep the revs up at 5000 or it would stall. "Beside the great physical similarity, Jacques reminded people of his father in many small gestures which had been typical of Gilles."

The Burattis insisted he began slowly again, "first learning how to change gear and brake." Jacques set off between the cones and tyres with "great energy" and clearly had skill. (Melanie did not venture

Imola, September 1985, getting ready for the beginning. Joann, Melanie, Jacques, Luigi Buratti (Autosprint).

31

into the Formula 4.) This induction completed, they gave Jacques three laps of the full Grand Prix circuit in the racing car, albeit with two saloons parallel in front of it and strict orders to remain behind them!

The *Autosprint* reporter, in one saloon with Joann, wrote: "We start. Jacques follows us about 10 metres behind. On his helmet I see the Maple Leaf and through the visor I see his eyes. We accelerate towards Tamburello [in Formula 1 a flat-out curving corner] which at the speed we were doing — 100, 110kph — looks almost like a straight piece of road. As we descend towards Tosa I can't help thinking of Gilles and the dreadful way he went off just here in 1980 . . ."

Massimo Buratti sat in the boot of the other saloon, its lid open, gesticulating instructions to Jacques — *"slow, move over a bit more to this side, move over a bit more to that side, change gear now."*

Towards day's end Jacques told the Burattis it had been "beautiful, beautiful, beautiful!" to which Joann responded "but he has to go back to college" — meaning concentrate on his studies, not this. Towards day's end, too, someone murmured to Joann that the children had shown aptitude. "Yes, I have seen that, unfortunately."

She spoke of them in the most honest, direct way. "Jacques is very similar to Gilles, not only physically but also — and especially — in his personality. He is strong-willed in the same way and as single-minded as Gilles was. When he sets himself a goal he doesn't give up until he has reached it. For this reason I am sure he will compete in kart races, although I will oppose him as long as I can.

"Melanie is more flexible. She is more like me. Given the way things are I can only hope that at least one of them will give up the idea of racing, but to compete in karts is not really dangerous. There are very few serious accidents. What frightens me is the way Jacques approaches any sport. Tennis, for instance. He doesn't want to practice because it isn't dangerous. He prefers to ski — downhill, obviously — do moto cross or whatever is risky. Gilles used to say that danger was part of his life, his son has made those words a tenet of his life and this is what worries me."

Soon enough there would be more to worry her.

There's an anecdote that subsequently Jacques drove a kart under the supervision (in general terms) of Tambay, who set him a test (again in general terms) by going round on a kart in front of him.

Plenty of instructions for Melanie (Luigi Buratti).

The face in the driving mirror, Imola (Luigi Buratti).

The Burattis lay hands on the roll bar, Zoboli poses, Jacques contemplates (Luigi Buratti).

Group photograph, Imola. Roberto Nosetto leans on the roll bar, Paolo Moruzzi has a blue sweater slung over his shoulders, Luigi Buratti has his arms round the shoulders of Vittorio Zoboli and Joann. Melanie is in the car, Jacques in the kart (Luigi Buratti).

"Jacques stayed happily on my tail and didn't make any mistakes." Former drivers like Tambay, with all their experience, notice what may be hidden from the eye of the casual spectator: kart control, self control, balance, accuracy, braking distance, demeanour, *nuances*.

In future, as Joann's objections remained firm, Tambay would counsel that if she forbade Jacques the chance of a career in racing before he became 18 (as legally she could) she'd lose the close relationship with him and he'd do it anyway. Tambay counselled further that the best course was to guide Jacques so that he started properly; and that is what Tambay would do. He told me: "I'm going to have a little bit of reserve and pudeur (modesty) about my role, because I never pushed. I gave advice — but pushed, no. I trust you know what I mean." Tambay is a gentleman in the true sense of that word — if you could pick your own godfather, he'd be impeccable. He explains what he does mean: when somebody gains the adulation and the fame, many others claim to have been central — whether they have or not, and no matter to what degree — and he has no wish for anything like that. He did exactly what he did, not more or less, and did what he knew was right. Uncle Jacques Villeneuve would do the same.

Quietly it began, and deliberately so, one Villeneuve wanting to protect another Villeneuve from the onrush which the name of the third Villeneuve would bring. To avoid confusion, I refer to Gilles' brother as Jacques (Snr) and Gilles' son as Jacques (Jnr). You'll see why.

All three Villeneuves were, at their differing times, graduates of the Jim Russell Driving School at Mont Tremblant, Quebec. And excellent advertisements for the school they all turned out to be. Jacques (Snr) was 1980 and 1981 Formula Atlantic Champion, 1983 Can-Am Champion, and experienced in IndyCars. He tried, and failed, to qualify for three Formula 1 Grands Prix in the early 1980s for Arrows/RAM.

The Burattis in their Bologna workshop, 1996 (Author).

Vince Laughran of the school knew Jacques (Snr) well. "He called us one day in 1986 and said 'listen, I want to put my nephew through the school, what do you think?' I said 'fantastic, a wonderful idea.' I believe Jacques (Jnr) and the family were over here visiting and between them it was sort of 'what do you think?' 'yeah, why not?' — very low key. Jacques (Snr) said 'no pressure on the kid' and I said 'sure, it's between you and us.'"

Laughran had "not met Jacques (Jnr) before. There was no fanfare. He struck me as quiet, reserved, like most any other 15-year-old fellow. He did not give the impression of a youngster who was aggressive and eager to go racing. He did give the appearance of someone who'd try something which might have been at the suggestion of his uncle. He was kind of taking it all in, an attentive student. That was, perhaps, the most impressive thing. I'm trying to say this as diplomatically as possible: you get a 15-year-old, any 15-year-old, to sit down for an hour-and-a-half to do *anything* and that's hard. He was able to concentrate. We were amazed at that. Maybe it came from his karting."

Maybe it just came from him.

Mont Tremblant, home of the Canadian Grand Prix in 1968 and 1970, once represented "pretty much the spirit, the hub of racing over here. Now, obviously, that's become the Grand Prix at Montreal."

The school used Formula Ford 1600 Van Diemens — "the basic schooling car, the basic entry-level formula car" — and approached their business with subtlety. "We ran a trial day, just getting your feet wet, and a full introductory programme which lasted three days. This is the programme he attended." Here is the subtlety. "We sit the fellow in the car right away and do classroom later. We've noticed over the years that there is an awful lot of apprehension, so our way of working is *let's sit him in the car and get that over with, let's break the ice, let's start driving at 9.0 in the morning.* Those who think they're good might find out they aren't and those who are timid find out there's not so much to be alarmed about.

"They get in the car and discover it has three pedals on the floor [like any other car]. OK, they have a little problem because there is no synchromesh but off they go and afterwards that makes the classroom part so much more absorbing. If you try the classroom first, every boy is waiting to drive and their minds wander. We've also discovered over the years that with the classroom first there's a bit of 'yes, sure,' 'oh yeah, sure,' 'I'll show you,' but when you put them in the car right away it's like a severe levelling process. Certainly when they've driven and had lunch and gone into the classroom you have *very* attentive students ready for teaching.

We were all talking that way: gosh it's amazing how this kid can concentrate

"The circuit is a 2.65 mile road course with 11 race corners. We have a club circuit too, which doesn't really lose any corners, only a loop. We use the club circuit for the bulk of the programme and finish up on the Grand Prix circuit. In the three days we try to give pupils some 150 laps. We take the pressure away by familiarisation laps, pace laps, warm-up laps and cool-off laps, and clock the student for the remaining 100 or 110. Jacques had endurance, he didn't tire and he was in shape. He'd ski-ed and done karts.

"The most impressive thing was his ability to concentrate and his ability to absorb what the instructor was telling him. If you are speaking to a 15-year-old telling him about weight transfer and turning too soon and turning too late and the slip angles, it's like talking to a 15-year-old about physics and geometry: hard to keep their attention. We were impressed by how he could go out and try to implement what the instructor had told him and often achieve that 100 per cent."

Amplifying this Laughran adds: "Jacques can sit down and work through problems. He is a great test driver, he can work with engineers, he can work with just about anybody," as he rapidly proved in testing with the F1 Williams so many years later.

"Jacques (Jnr) stayed at a local hotel, no fuss, and Jacques (Snr) had said 'no press' but it went so well we brought his favourite journalist — who'd known Gilles — and a staff photographer from the local paper and he took some pictures. Jacques (Jnr) had been among a bunch of fellows and probably half of them didn't know who he was. In those days the course cost around 1200, 1300 Canadian dollars but I think I did it as a favour to Jacques (Snr), who was around the entire three days and was playing, in my estimation, the perfect role.

"Obviously he couldn't play the father but he was playing the role of the father at the racing school: watching, not trying to teach him. He went to the corners because he knows what he is looking at. He's a guy that's raced IndyCars, for crying out loud! He *knows*. For the most part, however, he was laid back, had lunch with the nephew, got him a Coke if he needed something to drink or whatever; a good parental role.

"At the end of the three days, we were all pretty much impressed. Even Jacques (Snr) was impressed. 'Jeez, my nephew knows how to drive, my nephew can do these things.' We were all talking that way: *gosh it is amazing how this kid can concentrate*."

Laughran adds that Jacques (Jnr) was very much his own person, and everyone noticed this, including his uncle. "I don't think Jacques (Snr) started off with his expectation of *here's another Gilles Villeneuve*. No, he didn't, even if [soon enough] other people did. I shouldn't say the kid was amazing because that makes it sound too easy, particularly when you're talking about a 15-year-old who'd done a little bit of karting, but he was very good, he switched on."

A reporter, David Hatter, writing in *Formula 2000*, quoted Gilbert Pednault, the school's chief instructor, as saying: "He has natural car control. Taking into account that he's only just turned 15 and has hardly ever driven a street car, I would say he's the best student I have ever seen. One doesn't want to get carried away by the Villeneuve name, but it's mind-boggling. It must be genetics."

On the final day of the course, reportedly a soggy day in late July, Jacques (Snr) walked the circuit with a video camera as Jacques (Jnr) went round five or six seconds quicker than any of the other nine drivers in the class. The film is no longer a family affair. It belongs to posterity. "I guess racing is in his blood," Snr said. Joann was not there but the grandparents, Seville and Georgette, watched from the control tower.

Seville told Hatter: "I hope he does what he wants to do and I hope he does it well, although it will be hard to fill the shoes of his father. You're working with a tool where there is always danger, but

Right *At the Jim Russell School* (Daniel du Plessis/Canapress).

Jacques in action at the Jim Russell School, Mont Tremblant, July 1986 (Daniel du Plessis/Canapress).

you can't think about the darkness all the time."

The magazine quoted Jacques as saying the danger "doesn't bother me so much, I don't think about it" and reported he was "adamant" he wanted to drive Formula 1, preferably with Ferrari. You could certainly forgive any 15-year-old for expressing such sentiments but somehow it all reads like the enactment of a ritual. It was in the genes, it was in the blood, Formula 1, Ferrari — these sound suspiciously like the sort of questions people would ask and the sort of responses people were looking for.

Hatter concluded with this lovely paragraph: "As Pednault presents Jacques his diploma at the end of the three-day course, the other students are asking for his autograph. He is already getting more attention than many drivers receive in a lifetime. And the Villeneuve clan gathers around to congratulate and applaud him. Just one person is missing to complete the happy family portrait."

Well, two. Joann wasn't there either.

The most significant aspect — apart from the fact that he could actually drive and the inevitable references to Gilles — was the autograph hunting. He was famous by proxy, not by achievement. Perhaps it was good to face this so early and begin to accommodate it. There would be a lot, lot more of this.

The introduction to racing through a driving school can be as much the end of a career as the beginning. A youngster may discover he (and it is predominantly boys who attend) simply doesn't like racing or he's no good at it. He may have been given the course as a present and regard it as no more than that. He may be frightened, whether he admits it or not. He (or more accurately his parents) may be intimidated by the sheer cost of *any* further career in motorsport; and so on. There are many obstacles, right from the start.

Conversely, the youngster may discover the elixir of life and find himself needing more and more, the obstacles becoming challenges. That's solid grounding because as a career grows there will always be obstacles and, by a series of jungle initiation tests, the growing man will have to surmount them as they come at him. This holds true all the way to IndyCars or Formula 1 and their respective Championships. Maybe one core value of the school is that it kick-starts the process of separating those who want to go home from those who want to be World Champion. In the case of Jacques Villeneuve, the answer was at hand — if not already, then soon after.

A man called Richard Spenard had worked at the Russell School before setting up his own at Shannonville, about an hour and a half's drive from Toronto. This school was a further stage, running Formula 2000 cars. In 1987 "Jacques came to spend the summer," Spenard says. "We had a mechanics' training programme, a trade-off between manual work and racing where, in return for the work a pupil did in the garage, he was learning to drive and doing our series of tests and courses and practice. I have to admit Jacques didn't work very much. Some do, he didn't!"

Subsequently *Autosprint* carried an article by Villeneuve under the headline:

I HAVE CONTRACTED THE FAMILY VIRUS
(Mi ha contagiato un virus familiare)

The word virus has a hard meaning in English and perhaps it was intended to be softer in the article, perhaps not. Whatever,

41

Villeneuve explained that he travelled to Canada for summer holidays in 1985 — a year before the Russell School — when Uncle Jacques allowed him to try some of his cars and "I realised I had been infected."

Spenard was already acquainted with the family.

Jacques (Jnr) said "this man [Spenard] was impressed, seeing as I drove my uncle's Lamborghini Countach — I hope the Canadian police never find out! — and he said he would allow me onto a course. People might think all I had to do was go to my mother to get the money but it wasn't like that at all. She opposed it and said it was much more important to continue my studies. An application form for the school arrived at home. She said nothing and threw it away hoping it was only a summer infatuation of mine. I'd guessed the form might finish like that so I'd asked for a copy to be sent to the college. By Christmas, and after a thousand complications, I obtained permission but not the money. Fortunately the owner of the school took me on as a mechanic and, working at that, I paid for my driving lessons."

Spenard remembers "he was playful, quiet, a little lazy, didn't like to get his hands dirty. As a matter of fact, there's a funny story. Most of the kids were working on the race cars but, because he didn't like to get his hands dirty, we ended up having him paint the garage! The guys realised that the garage was painted by Jacques Villeneuve so they're going to keep it that way for a long time.

"Shannonville is a road course two and a half miles long, very flat and similar to Snetterton in England. We were equipped with Formula 2000 cars and it's a big circuit, a good training circuit for Formula 2000. I'd known Gilles well, I was a team-mate of his and obviously I'd known the son — I'd had to baby-sit. He was just a typical boy, a great kid, playing with his sister all the time. He was seven or eight, very playful, taking a lot of his father's time, nothing unusual.

"In 1987 I knew he was coming to Canada and we said 'well, it would be good for us to have him, he has a good name.' I had to go to Europe anyway, so I sat down with his mother in Monaco and made a

Right *Uncle Jacques keeps a watchful eye, and records for posterity, at a kart race outside Montreal, August 1986. Villeneuve won but was relegated to second for bumping another kart!* (Robert Eardley/Canapress).

Villeneuve, number 3, on his way to fourth place in a race at Sanair Speedway, Quebec, August 1986 (Paul-Henri Talbot/Canapress).

deal for him to come and spend the summer with us. Of course he was so young then that his mother wanted to be sure he was in good hands. He struck me as spoilt (deep chuckle), you know, definitely not like Gilles."

Let's be careful about spoilt because, in this context, it has two mean-ings: given everything you want, or having a comfortable upbringing.

44

Spenard, I sense, means the latter — something quite different.

"Well, he had been raised in Monaco. Obviously he didn't have to worry too much about anything in his life, whereas his father had had a very different upbringing; but otherwise you could see he had some natural talent. It was not polished at all. He was a spur-of-the-moment driver, quick on one lap, going off on the second lap.

45

Left *Sanair Speedway, and Joann looks happy* (Paul-Henri Talbot/Canapress).

Basically he was not into it, he wasn't sure that that was what he wanted to do. He was there at the school, it was easy for him to be there and he had fun."

There was some talk he wanted to be a ski racer.

"Maybe that's why he was confused a bit. He wasn't necessarily a superstar but definitely one of the good drivers we had, although not extremely spectacular [the inevitable comparison]. Because of his age he had no experience of driving on ordinary roads but he was still fairly quick. At the beginning you could see he had a talent to do that. What he lacked was the discipline to be consistently quick and to work at it."

People expected him to be like his father?

"Yes."

But clearly he wasn't.

"That's right. Actually, I think he has a natural talent from his father but he has a different style. I believe it is a bit of a combination."

Not just to win races but championships.

"Right, yes and . . . survive."

This is still, however, 1987, and Villeneuve is 16. "He was learning with us, he was progressing, oh yes, no question, no question, sure he was, but you know he was not much better than everybody else."

Yet.

• CHAPTER TWO •

Go your
own way

THE BEGINNING OF Jacques Villeneuve's racing career was curious, for two reasons. In 1988, at 17 he was a year too young to obtain an international competition licence in Italy or Canada so he applied to Andorra, the mountainous 'country' between France and Spain where he could get one, albeit with parental permission. Residential qualifications? My tentative enquiries suggest that Andorra is more like a maze than a country, with 'official' residences and perhaps privileged residences too. Andorrans are natural entrepreneurs and to qualify you might need only, as someone suggested, "spend a minimum of time here." Certainly the staff of the Automobil Club remember seeing the young chap often, and insist he had friends there. Anyway, from the maze emerged one driving licence in the name of J. Villeneuve.

The maze was not so simple, however. Reportedly the "legal problems" of a licence were solved by the Canadian Automobile Federation who sent permission for Villeneuve to compete because his first race — in touring cars at Pergusa, Italy — would be national "with the participation of foreigners" rather than an international event. The difference might seem minimal but clearly wasn't. It does explain why his nationality was sometimes given as AND for Andorra and sometimes CAN for Canada.

The second curiosity is that Villeneuve entered racing via touring cars, although single-seaters are the much more usual route. At the end of 1988 he drove three rounds of the Italian Touring Championship in an Alfa Romeo 33 for a team called Salerno Corse. The venture was backed by *Autosprint* and he told them: "This year I'll enter the racing world seriously in the Alfa 33 and next year I'd like to do single-seaters. I don't know if I'll compete in Formula 3 or Formula Opel Lotus. I hope to be able to establish good relationships with the other drivers, especially the young ones, because although my name is Villeneuve I'm just a boy like them who, when going to sleep, thinks of nothing but cars and races. I must also keep the promise I made to my mother to continue studying until I graduate."

Jacques was only 17 and would now have to confront The Name and the comparisons

He tested the Alfa at Vallelunga, a circuit which has been described as "high in the hills above Rome, surrounded by vineyards and rolling countryside." Initially he covered about 20 laps, quickly finding the racing line and constantly improving his time by a tenth of a second a lap. The comparison could not be resisted: *Autosprint* reported that "he showed great style, like his father." This same day he also tried a small single-seater and, searching for its limit, spun into the tyre wall. Neither he nor the car were damaged. It must be re-stated that Jacques Villeneuve was only 17 and would now have to confront The Name and the comparison head on. Moreover he'd meet experienced drivers like Mauro Baldi (Formula 1 from 1982–1985), Johnny Cecotto (1983–1984) and Roberto Ravaglia. The Pergusa race was over two legs of one hour each and Villeneuve finished tenth. That was 25 September. Two weeks later, at Monza, more Formula 1 men — Riccardo Patrese and Nicola Larini — came in amidst a "massive entry of 135." One report says that "the impetuous Jacques Villeneuve took out Maurizio Milla's Toyota on lap 4." At Imola two weeks after that he finished fourteenth.

"I did three races, but I don't call that racing," Villeneuve would say. "It was just touring around. It was the worst car I ever drove. I finished the first race, but just by taking the kerbs the car was all

September 1988. Villeneuve prepares to drive the Alfa Romeo 33 for Salerno Corse (Autosprint).

smashed in. I prefer to forget all about it."

Julian Thomas, a journalist who reported the fledgeling career, reaches for the perspective. "Basically, he was given a leg up by Alfa Romeo. *Autosprint* organised a competition for young drivers in Alfa Romeos and Jacques was given the opportunity to do the last three races. Absolute disaster. He smashed the car up virtually every time he drove it and it had to go back to the bodyshop. Why give him a leg up? Because of his name, I suppose. He'd been helped by Patrick Tambay before and Patrick had said 'OK, if you really want to go into motorsport then do it seriously' and the name Villeneuve still meant a lot in Italy."

He left Beau Soleil and moved to Italian Formula 3 in 1989. Yula de Meyer says that in the autumn of 1988 "Jacques went every other weekend to do the races in the Alfa Romeo. He asked to combine that with his studies and we accepted. Three races weren't too many, although he'd leave here on the Friday, do the race over the weekend and not be able to return until the Monday — because we're in the mountains there are no train connections after 9.0 on Sunday evenings. He'd come back tired, taut, and then do classes Tuesday, Wednesday and Thursday.

"In February 1989 he showed us the Formula 3 programme. It was virtually every weekend and we said no, 'you must choose.' It was the last two years of the baccalaureate (the exam leading to university), which were important. He reflected and said 'no, I prefer to do the races.' He could have combined the two — he was capable of that — but he'd have needed a big desire, a lot of desire and he'd have had to make a lot of sacrifices. I believe he was too young to make these sacrifices. So he chose the races. It was a pity, but that's how he left us."

(When he paid a social call to the college in December 1995 the de Meyers pointed out that he had no qualifications and "what happens when you're 40?" I sense that they don't quite realise he'll be a multi-millionaire long before then, which is more than enough qualification. I find their question protective, traditional and charming. Pierre de Meyer told me in 1996 "I still regret he didn't do the bacc.")

He joined the PreMa team, experienced practitioners in Italian Formula 3. Tambay "had nothing to do with him going into Italian

F3. A guy in Monte Carlo, who I think was a lawyer, thought his name would be very good for his own promotion, I would imagine, and put the package together. [I'm sure that Tambay is too polite to say that he might have counselled against Italian F3, if for no other reason than The Name.] Jacques was very young, had to go to Andorra to get a licence but that was only on the impulse of the Italian guy . . ."

Let's not get into that particular maze again. Other mazes await us.

Before that, let's hear Angelo Rosin, technical director of PreMa, then based in Vicenza, a city near Venice. "It's not the usual route in a career to *start* in Formula 3. All he'd done was a little bit of karting. His level was not a professional level, not even international races. It wasn't a real karting career. Suddenly he came to Formula 3 because there were people around him who believed that that name and that boy could be good in a promotional sense. In fact this happened.

Driving it (Autosprint).

When we went in Formula 3 there were a lot of fans around who were Gilles Villeneuve fans, but also young people came — teenagers — because it was the son of Gilles.

"PreMa had already had one driver who was a Camel Italy driver and they believed Jacques could be good for them. It was natural. At Camel was a big businessman called Giovanni Russi — he was the centre of Camel Italy at that time — and he believed not only in the name but also in Jacques Villeneuve, driver. However, nobody had any idea what the future would hold.

"Initially, it was difficult for PreMa to accept this situation because in a racing car Jacques was nothing! He knew nothing about racing cars, he knew nothing about races! Camel paid for Jacques so for PreMa it meant money. You have to understand, however, that a team doesn't just live on money. It also lives on results. Anyway we got a driver who knew nothing, it was difficult, and it was all a question I asked myself. It was however a challenge to take a complete novice and make something of him. And it was more difficult because he was so young. When he first tested, in December of 1988, he didn't even know how to use the gears! He learnt step by step.

"And the first time he drove in the rain, he was afraid that the visor of his helmet would steam up from the inside. He took a piece of black tape and stuck it on his nose and cheeks. Why? He'd seen that was what his father did to prevent humidity [by channelling the exhaled air downwards, away from the visor] and so he did it. Everybody was amazed! Virtually nobody does this, but he didn't know. It was funny. However it worked because he didn't have a problem.

"Of course, other drivers have started in Formula 3 but an aspect of the challenge was to take a novice with a very important name, although the pressure was higher. In fact this was the real challenge. We foresaw that whatever pressure was on the team would be on Jacques too. He always had a lot of journalists and photographers as well as fans around him at the tracks.

"Camel didn't cover the entire budget of the team, so it was an investment which PreMa made in Villeneuve, and it was hard because, on what money we had, it wasn't possible to do a lot of testing. He only did a small amount of kilometres in the winter. Normally a driver does a lot in his first year in order that it's easier for

Trying a Formula Fiat Abarth single-seater, 1988 (Autosprint).

Angelo Rosin and Simone Battistella of the PreMa team (Author).

them to have a feeling for the car. Jacques was really, really young and it was a game for him. He was clear-thinking, and direct with people. It created a good relationship between Jacques, me and the guys in the team. When he came to Vicenza he didn't sleep in an hotel, he stayed at my house in my son's bedroom.

"There were hard situations with the press. If he didn't go well in qualifying, everybody was asking 'why, what's wrong, what's the matter?' The whole team tried to undramatise everything. In Italy, more than in other countries, the pressure of The Name was strong, it was heavy."

Yes, the media descended. In answer to my question *what sort of an impression did Villeneuve make that first season?* Thomas replied: "Zero basically. He didn't even qualify for the first three races, didn't get any points at all during the season. He had a lot of hangers-on, let's say, people trying to influence him because of his name and because of his background. He gave the impression of being, let's say, cynical. Well, not quite, but very calm about things. Not the warmest character, certainly, when I knew him. We got on quite well. I found him a nice guy but quite cold, quite analytical. That helped him develop as a driver because technically he was pretty damn good. He could give a lot of feed-back about the car because he'd worked as a mechanic [at Spenard!].

"I think he was nonplussed by all the attention surrounding him. The Italian newspapers sent all their big names to interview him. He'd say 'well, I'm just starting my career. I can't say whether I'll drive for Ferrari one day or not.' They wanted all that out of him. He definitely wasn't one of those who want to exploit their name, he simply wanted to be regarded as another Formula 3 driver. He found the pressure which came from the level of expectation hard. Newspapers like *La Gazzetta dello Sport* [the leading daily consecrated to sport] gave, at the best of times, about five lines to an Italian Formula 3 race. They'd say *Victory to Alessandro Zanardi; did not qualify, Villeneuve* and that would be it. They were singling him out.

"Another problem he had in 1989 was messing up the starts the whole time. Quite often he might be near the front of the grid but he

Right *Italian Formula 3 in Camel colours* (Julian Thomas).

just couldn't start at all. He'd slip the clutch and stall. That was inexperience."

La Stampa journalist Christiano Chiavegato says that "1989 was a bad season. The car wasn't very good and he made many mistakes and broke the car. I interviewed him at Monza, the fifth race, on 25 June. He was — and is — a nice man, he spoke excellent Italian and he was like a businessman: very, very professional, very, very elegant in speech and behaviour, not like a driver! When he spoke, he was impressive, saying polite things about everything, his life, his mother, his father. He said he didn't have a good feeling with his mother because he was racing and she was against it.

I'd say 'his father is his father but this guy is different, the complete opposite'

"The first time he raced everyone wanted to know about him because it was the son of Villeneuve but after a time people forgot because he wasn't very good. I think he found it difficult. He had a good sponsor [Camel, to pay for the drive] but no money [as in spending money]. People said *he's not so good, not so talented, not like his father.* When I interviewed him he said 'I am Jacques Villeneuve, not Gilles Villeneuve' and I must say that impressed me. Officially he doesn't like the comparison although I don't know if that's true in private. He said 'I want to be different from my father' but again I don't know if he dreams of being like him.

"The Italian Championship was too hard for him that first season. He was so young and there were many pressures in the team. He had a big psychological problem, maybe because he was so young. He was a strong driver, quick, but he didn't know the technique of driving. For example, he'd be fast in the fast corners but brake in the wrong place for the slow corners — that was lack of technique. He had to learn it. When the PreMa team looked at the telemetry they saw he made a lot of mistakes."

Wouldn't it have been easy to quit?

"No, no! I think he was deeply interested in a motor racing career and he knew he could become good."

A driver called Mauro Martini watched with mounting disquiet.

"When Jacques started, I think I was one of the few who believed in his possibilities. Everyone was expecting him to win immediately but at that moment the Italian Formula 3 Championship was highly competitive. It was hard for a beginner, plus he'd never raced a single-seater before, plus he had the pressure of The Name. Too much pressure. Because I understood how difficult it all was, I knew his results were not so bad. When he'd finish tenth I knew it was bloody good but everyone was saying it wasn't good enough.

"I told the journalists 'you have to give him more time, you can't expect the guy to just come along and win races.' They'd say 'yes, but his father, his father.' I'd say 'his father was his father, this guy is different, *obviously* he's different. He is completely the opposite of his father. He's got The Name and the face, probably, but his driving style is so different. He is so accurate in his preparation.' I remember he'd get pretty upset to have all these people around connecting him to his father. He'd say 'look, I'm *Jacques* Villeneuve.' I have to tell you this: some of the time people mistakenly [and helplessly, no doubt] called him Gilles. He'd say 'hey, it's Jacques . . .'

"Gilles had been one of my favourite drivers and I spoke many times with Jacques because I wanted to know more about Gilles. He couldn't tell me a lot. He didn't know his father so well."

Julian Thomas offers a different perspective. "He was a disaster at first. A lot of people used to laugh and say 'oh, you'd be better off skiing' because he seemed to be a young hooligan (chuckle), quite long hair, this devil-may-care attitude plus the way he drove. I mean he was very, very aggressive but always under control. His father often gave the impression of not being under control. Bear in mind, however, that when Jacques started, money was flowing freely in Italy and 56 drivers were entered for the racing. You had to have two repechages (eliminating races) and a final! I remember 1989 as a superb season of racing."

In May Villeneuve entered the Monaco Formula 3 race which traditionally supports the Grand Prix and is a real chance for promising drivers to impress the Formula 1 moguls. He did not qualify. *Autosport* wrote: "Jacques Villeneuve, son of Gilles, missed the cut by 0.693 of a second, albeit showing that he can learn early, this being only his third F3 appearance." His best time, one minute 41.274, wasn't at all bad in the circumstances even compared to pole, one minute 37.810, by Italian Antonio Tamburini.

He didn't qualify for the next race, Varano, but finished tenth two weeks later at Pergusa, a fast track — the first race he had qualified for. "He showed something very, very good," Rosin says. "He was going well but at the chicane just before the pit lane entrance he braked too late. He understood instantly that he couldn't get through the chicane so he drove into the pit lane really fast! We thought he had a problem with the car and was pitting. He ran past us down the pit lane using it like the track and didn't lose a place! Next lap he didn't make the mistake . . ."

Reflecting on 1989, Villeneuve would say: "I was lucky because PreMa is one of the best teams. The first year was really good for experience. I was one second off the pace for most of the year. That was good for learning: to be one second off the pace and still have to push hard to get qualified on the last row."

Rosin remembers that "every time we went to a track where we had been before, he drove better, his times improved. He showed good quality, but everything needed to be developed. The qualities were of the kind that could make him a good driver and it was a question of waiting for him to grow. He was better on the fast tracks. Slow corners were more difficult for him to learn."

In the second year he showed improvement, with a second place at Binetto in July. Martini regarded that as proof of Villeneuve's quality. "Still everybody was saying 'oh, second season, he should win.' He was a kid! He's a kid now [1995], so you can imagine how he was five, six years ago!"

Rosin says "Binetto? It was only a question of time before he achieved something like that. Binetto is a really short and slow track and he had learnt it."

Christiano sums it up: "He started to become better."

Thomas sums it up: "He almost won at Binetto but he still seemed to be very cold. There's an example that I remember. His team-mate Giuseppe Bugatti had quite a violent accident at Varano and it left a mark on the other drivers. A lot of them really didn't want to go out and practice but Jacques went out no problem at all. A lot of people thought this was quite cynical of him."

Right *Concentrating* (Julian Thomas).

Left *Speed was no problem but the slow corners were* (Julian Thomas).

Formula 3 is intrinsically cut-and-thrust. Reporting the race at Varano, Thomas wrote "when the flag dropped, Jacques Villeneuve, with a dead engine, caused havoc on the tight grid with cars all over the place and even on the grass . . ."

Mind you, Villeneuve 'won' the final race of 1990 but was penalised a minute for jumping the start, relegating him to four-teenth. In three seasons of Italian Formula 3 it was the closest he came to winning.

Fragments of the cut-and-thrust, 1990: he qualified well at Vallelunga but was soon overtaken for third and retired with mechanical problems . . . at Pergusa he worked a steady course to

Explaining what happened after crashing at Monaco, 1991 (Paul Velasco/Canapress).

sixth and his first Italian F3 point . . . at Imola he set fastest lap and was narrowly beaten for fourth . . . at Monza he and Domenico Schiattarella banged wheels and went off . . . at Misano he became lost in a great deal of barging . . . at Monza a duel with Eugenio Visco ended when Villeneuve spun on the final lap . . . we've already had the havoc at Varano.

Villeneuve would reflect that "the second year everything went much easier. I was qualifying on the third row at most races. I don't know why, but I was a second faster without pushing harder. After one year, everything came better in my head, I guess. Everything was easier, and maybe I was more relaxed."

He stayed a third year. Of it Thomas says "he was one of the pre-season favourites for the Championship but the team goofed. They started off with Reynards, and Ralts were dominating all over Europe. After three races they changed to Ralts but by then the season was compromised. He got pole positions and was three times on the podium."

Did you see something in him?

"Yes, definitely. I thought he'd go a long way. Somehow I thought he couldn't fail."

Why do you say that?

"He just seemed to have the right sort of attitude towards racing: not necessarily the cynical, ruthless guy but very, very cool, calm and collected. Italians are very excitable about things. Even a die-hard Formula 1 guy like Gianni Morbidelli [in from 1990 to 1995] still doesn't strike me as a champion though he won Formula 3. There was something special in Villeneuve. OK, maybe he didn't cover himself in glory in Italy but that, I suspect, is due to the character of Italians who were expecting a lot more from him."

Fragments of the cut-and-thrust, 1991. At Imola he took pole but made a poor start and was "overwhelmed," finishing fourth . . . at Monza he was described as "rapidly improving" and took pole again but "once again he messed up the start," and finished second . . . later at Monza he took pole again and made another mess of the start, recovered, led but on the final lap a Brazilian clipped him, sending them both onto the gravel at the second chicane. "I got out of the sandtrap and still managed to finish third," Villeneuve would say. "I was so disappointed that when I crossed the finish line I banged the

The beginning. Villeneuve prepares to go karting at Imola, September 1985 (Autosprint).

Luigi Buratti makes sure the seat fits (Autosprint).

Action, Imola (Luigi Buratti).

The paternal presence of Buratti with Jacques and Melanie (Luigi Buratti).

Right *Joann relieved, Imola* (Autosprint).

Right *In the wet at Jim Russell* (Daniel du Plessis/Canapress).

A family affair. With Uncle Jacques at the Jim Russell School, Mont Tremblant (Daniel du Plessis/ Canapress).

Striding towards the Alfa Romeo and a whole career, autumn 1988
(Autosprint).

Yes, he did look young in Italian Formula 3, didn't he? (Studio 83).

Right *A couple of years later he'd changed completely* (Studio 83).

Grandparents Seville and Georgette watch from the control tower at Mont Tremblant (Daniel du Plessis/Canapress).

Learning the hard way. Qualifying, Pergusa, 1989 (Studio 83).

Exploring Monaco, 1991 (Studio 83).

Leading through the chicane at Monza, 1991 (Studio 83).

Going through the chicane at Monza four years later (ICN U.K. Bureau).

Listening (Julian Thomas).

Trois Rivieres, 1992, and the entry into Formula Atlantic. Note for the races he wears contact lenses (Michel Gravel/ Canapress).

A family affair further on. Jacques leads Uncle Jacques at Trois Rivieres! (Bernard Brault/ Canapress).

Tony Cicale takes note of everything (Frank Gunn/ Canapress).

Toronto, with girlfriend Sandrine Gros d'Aillon (Robert Laberge/Canapress).

Laguna Seca and eleventh place would be good enough for the championship (Paul Sakuma/Canapress).

Left *Indianapolis, 28 May, 1995* (Al Behrman/Canapress).

The 1996 team: Villeneuve with Frank Williams, and (below) alongside partner Damon Hill (ICN U.K. Bureau).

steering wheel and broke my hand." At Mugello reportedly he took a driver called Paolo Coloni off.

Villeneuve also competed in the Formula 3 races at Monaco in May and Macau in November. At Monaco he qualified well. *Autosport* wrote: "Prior knowledge of the track helped, and third slot [on the grid] was claimed by Jacques Villeneuve, much to the popular acclaim of those in the press room who still revere his late father, Gilles. Indeed, it was fitting that the young PreMa Racing driver should have been fastest for much of the session, this coming 10 years after Gilles' famous win in the main race." In the 1991 race Frenchman Laurent Daumet "became impatient with Villeneuve's pace, tipping both out with a hopeless dive into the chicane on lap 5 that saw others mounting the kerbs to avoid the entangled pair."

At Macau several Italians spun in qualifying but "the Italian contingent was bolstered by the rather more controlled performance of Jacques Villeneuve in the faster of the PreMa Racing Ralts. Schiattarella, a rival in the Italian series, had been drafted into the team and was rather less rapid, ending up nineteenth." The race was over two heats and in the first Villeneuve finished "a lonely ninth." He was eighth overall. The winner, incidentally, was David Coulthard. At Macau a leading Japanese team called TOM's Toyota had a word with Villeneuve about his immediate future.

Reflecting on 1991 Villeneuve would say "we just couldn't understand the car [the new Reynard]. We switched to the Ralt for the fourth race. We received the car one week before the race and didn't have any testing. It didn't go well. Then we had Monaco the week after. There it went better. My team was really surprised, because we qualified third. And then in the race some idiot French driver ran into me and we finished both our races at the chicane."

"In 1991," Rosin says, "there was a problem. We won the championship in 1990 with Roberto Calciago and a Reynard chassis, so we started the season with the Reynard '91. It was a mistake because the Reynard was slower than the Ralt. We decided to change to Ralt but that meant all the winter work was lost. That proved a real problem for Jacques because it's not easy for a driver to change chassis. The rest of the season was really hard but Jacques did well.

"PreMa wanted to make the jump into Formula 3000 with Jacques in 1992. It was before Macau. We contacted two different sponsors.

81

One was Camel and the other was Diesel Jeans. Camel however were not sure and at that stage Diesel Jeans were not close enough to us to sponsor a Formula 3000 effort so we lost time. Jacques had had an offer at Macau where he'd done a very, very good drive. Our engine was not competitive and other engines were faster but Jacques proved quicker than a lot of them. TOM's Toyota saw that and understood he was a really good driver. Also he had a good name for the promotional side.

"I wanted to have Jacques for one more year and try for the Formula 3 Championship — it would have been the last stage of the challenge and the culmination of a beautiful experience — or try 3000, but to go to Japan was the best choice for him. In Italy he was tired of this situation with Gilles and it was the right move for his career. It wasn't a game any more. I must be careful with that word and make a difference. Although it was a game he approached it professionally.

"For the first part of the first season the racing car was a game. But he discovered that he was fast in the second season — among the fastest drivers, always in the first six on the grid although he still didn't know much about racing. He was not used to races, the control you need, everything. Sometimes he'd make mistakes at the start, sometimes he crashed but what he did have was speed.

"I think that when he knew that, he thought about making it a profession, becoming a driver for life."

• CHAPTER THREE •

Home and away

IT COULD NOT sensibly go on. There are too many witnesses who agree that the pressure of The Name was much more than an irritant; it was a genuine handicap. Patrick Tambay says, "after three years, I think Jacques and the Italian guy who got him into racing parted company. Jacques was alone and a bit lost and he came to me to ask what he should do. He had options: stay in Italy or race Formula 3 in England. I seem to recall he had another offer, although I can't remember exactly what. He also had an opportunity to go to Japanese Formula 3.

"My suggestion was to go to Japan to get out of the environment of his name and the pressure of the Italian crowd. It would also get him out of the family environment, I should say, to be able to mature by himself and do this in Japan in an environment which would be hostile. He could learn over there and probably it would raise him to another plateau. This is exactly what he did. He went to Japan." Angelo Rosin feels Villeneuve chose Japan to escape the pressure of The Name.

Villeneuve has described it like this: "For 1992 we were supposed to do Formula 3000 with PreMa but the money was lacking. We also thought about doing another Formula 3 season but I'd had a good offer from TOM's Toyota when I was in Macau. I thought about it in Fuji, and after I got back to Europe I decided to go to Japan for two reasons. One, because it was TOM's Toyota, which might be good for the future, and because the F3 Championship is nearly as good as the Italian. It's better than the English, French and German. Two, I was tired of being in Europe."

Julian Thomas "wasn't surprised when he went to Japan. He'd had enough of Italian Formula 3. He hadn't won a race but I don't think he had much left to prove by staying. PreMa wanted to go to Formula 3000 with Camel Italy but Camel couldn't get the budget together so they parted ways."

Mauro Martini, then in Japanese Formula 3000, insists: "He didn't want to stay in Italy any more. He said he was really frustrated in Italy. He wanted a change because of the pressure of the press. He didn't want to be constantly known as the son of Gilles. He wanted to be known by his own name. At the end of 1991 he came to Fuji to do the international Formula 3 race after Macau. TOM's were looking for a driver and they got in touch with him. Because he knew I was driving in Japan, he called me and asked for information about Japan. I told him how to go about it and I told him he could get good money. He was excited about coming.

"When he arrived, people recognised him because of The Name but not to the same degree as in Italy. His father was a legend, a god in Italy. In Japan he was just a driver who'd died in Formula 1. Of course Gilles was famous but it was completely different. I think that helped Jacques because he grew up quicker. He rented a flat in Tokyo and was living by himself. I have to say he was spending a lot of money. He didn't care so much about the money! One day he went into a store and he bought a stereo, a television, everything for his flat. He spent like $10,000. We went around together."

What sort of a young man was he?

"He was still a kid. It was pretty funny because we could tell him whatever we wanted and he would believe it! He was a very, very nice guy and we remain good friends. Even if we don't make contact for a year it doesn't make any difference. He's such a good guy, such a nice guy and I am sure that if he wins the Formula 1 World Championship he won't change.

Right *Breakthrough into Formula Atlantic at Trois Rivieres, 1992* (Michel Gravel/Canapress).

It was fine, mum, it was fine (Michel Gravel/Canapress).

"It's difficult driving and racing in Japan. People in Europe don't understand how difficult — and not just Formula 3 but every category. The culture is so different, the way of living is different, they don't speak good English plus you have to get along with the Japanese mechanics and engineers and that's pretty tough, too. [In general] nobody helps you to get a good result because, of course, they don't want a foreigner to go there and win races. They want Japanese drivers to win. The Japanese are strange people. It is hard to get along with them and that's why, coming back to the main point, it is hard to drive and be competitive there. Jacques achieved it.

"You have to speak to the mechanics and engineers in a sort of English which is called Japlish. Sometimes I feel very stupid when I speak to the mechanics like this but, if not, they don't understand me [Martini is fluent in English]. Jacques had to do the same, had to use Japlish. Jacques is very good with languages and, for example, his Italian is perfect. He tried to learn Japanese but he didn't have enough time because he was only there for a year. I'm sure if he had

86

been there longer he would have become fluent. He's that good at picking up languages."

Folklore implies that Villeneuve would be partnered at TOM's by the Swede Rickard Rydell. "I was not his team-mate," Rydell says, "but I drove the same car he was driving. He had a works set-up from TOM's and I was driving for a private team. Myself, Jacques and Tom Kristensen [a Dane] all drove the same cars. I didn't know him at all before he came to Japan, no. He was a stranger.

"My first impression was that he was a little bit — well *quite* — laid back and was just there to have fun, really, not taking it seriously. He was always very relaxed and enjoyable to be with. In fact he was taking it seriously, yes, yes, for sure. It's always been a little bit of a game for him. We went round together on race weekends, Friday, Saturday, Sunday. Sometimes we'd play 10-pin bowling — a lot of the time, in fact — and sometimes we went to a karioke place. He sang and I sang . . ."

What did it sound like?

"Not too good. You wouldn't be too impressed really, but it was enjoyable."

What did you sing?

"All sorts, all kinds. There are always some songs that you know

Action, Trois Rivieres (Bernard Brault/Canapress).

and they've got all kinds of music there, so that was quite good. We didn't meet much during the week. He lived in Tokyo and I lived near Fuji, and I went back to Sweden when I could. He stayed in Japan the whole year."

Was it difficult to be competing against somebody and yet be friends with them?

"No, I have never had a problem with that. Some drivers have, some drivers don't like to get too close and next day go out and race and have one another off. And we became good friends, because out in Japan you are very much alone, you don't socialise too much with the Japanese. That's mostly because of the language. Some of the Japanese speak good English and you'd go out more with those people."

During the year, could you see him getting better?

"Yes, for sure. He learned a lot out there. He was maybe not the fastest of us but he did finish the races. It's difficult to say what sort of a driver he was. He was not at all spectacular or wild or anything, more like trying to finish the races."

The 1992 Japanese F3 season:

Round 1, Suzuka. Reportedly the new TOM's car wasn't as competitive as that of 1991 and Villeneuve nursed it to sixth. An Englishman, Anthony Reid, won.

Round 2, Tsukuba. Reid won again at this "tight and twisty" circuit. Villeneuve inherited fourth place when Kristensen was disqualified.

Round 3, Fuji. A hat-trick to Reid but this time Villeneuve inherited a great deal more than a single place. An Italian called Eugenio Visco led but was penalised a minute for jumping the start; Kristensen (third) and Rydell (fourth) were both found to have underweight cars — so Villeneuve, sixth, became third.

Round 4, Suzuka. The Formula 3 event accompanied a Japanese Formula 3000 race in which a driver called Hitoshi Ogawa crashed fatally after striking another car. In the F3 event, Reid won again while Villeneuve, sixth on the grid, worked a path through some bumping and barging at the start to be third and hold that to the end.

Between Suzuka and the next round, at Nishi-Sendai, Villeneuve returned to Europe to contest the Formula 3 support race at Monaco.

He drove for PreMa again and qualified sixth. "Compared to my TOM's in Japan, the Dallara feels like it had power steering," he said. *Autosport* inevitably wrote that "the young Canadian had no problems with the track, the scene of his father's victory in the Grand Prix 11 years ago." In the race, and into Mirabeau — the sharp right-hander and one of the very few overtaking places — Pedro Lamy lunged inside Robert Colciago and Villeneuve lunged, too: three abreast. "I took a chance," Villeneuve said. "If Colciago turned in I was in trouble, if not then fine." Colciago turned in, Villeneuve was in trouble and, the front wing reshaped, finished ninth.

In Japan it was mostly good people who couldn't afford to race in Europe

Round 5, Nishi-Sendai. Rydell took pole, Villeneuve alongside him on the front row. Villeneuve made the better start and defended the lead round this tortuous circuit (it had 15 corners) without making a mistake. Reid floundered over the circuit's bumps, could qualify no higher than eighth and retired when his car locked in third gear. This was the first victory of Villeneuve's career.

Round 6, Ti Circuit. Kristensen 'won' but was excluded when the airbox on his car was ruled illegal (his third exclusion this season). It promoted Rydell to victory and Villeneuve to third.

Round 7, Mine. Reid, who hadn't been to the circuit before, could have taken the championship here — with a win — and after wet qualifying was on the front row (Rydell pole). The Englishman led but couldn't pull away and a hungry pack, Villeneuve spearheading it, circled behind him. "It was match point for 10 laps," Reid said, "but right from the start I knew I was in trouble with the handling." Into turn one on lap 11 Villeneuve made his move and went through. Reid fell away and finished seventh. Villeneuve won it comfortably enough.

Round 8, Sugo. Reid took pole from Villeneuve and led. "Villeneuve's already slim chance of taking the honours was blown when Akira Ishikawa beat him for second place [after the green light]. Jacques was unhappy with his engine after a change following the warm-up, but he kept pushing. However, he ran wide on the grass

at one point allowing Kristensen to sneak through into third"
(*Autosport*).

Round 9, Suzuka. Teams were allowed to use their own fuel here,
as against taking it from a communal source. Elf provided TOM's
with a potent brew, the cars had new and superior suspensions and
were not to be caught. Villeneuve took pole but missed second gear
at the start so that Rydell seized the lead and didn't let it go. "I can't
remember it clearly," Rydell says, "but once I was in the lead it must
have been a boring race then! We were very evenly matched between
Tom Kristensen, Jacques and myself so if one car was ahead it tended
to win."

Round 10, Suzuka. Villeneuve took pole but again missed second
gear at the start, allowing Kristensen through. During the first lap he
bustled past Kristensen and accelerated to win it comfortably enough.
He'd scored points in every round.

What was the overall standard of driving like?

"Overall in Japan it has always been very, very good," Rydell says.
"Of course the last one or two years there are a lot less European
drivers out there, but when we were there in '92 we had seven or
eight European drivers in Formula 3 and 12 to 14 drivers in F3000 and
the standard was high. A lot of good drivers like Eddie Irvine were
produced. Mostly it's been good people who haven't had the money
to race in Europe. For sure, Jacques must have gone a lot better since
he left Japan from what I've seen. He's done a first rate good job. He
learnt in Japan but he's still learning and getting much better."

Between these two races at Suzuka, Villeneuve competed in a third
there: the Formula 3 non-championship event. This was a support to
the Japanese Grand Prix (where Damon Hill might have been trying
to qualify a deeply uncompetitive Brabham, but wasn't. Brabham,
absent, had run out of money two months before).

"A second-lap wheel-banging incident between Rydell, Tetsuya
Tanaka and Jacques Villeneuve saw the Canadian pitched off the
road. Jacques was unhurt but posted his first retirement of the year
after a string of top six finishes" (*Autosport*). "What happened?"
Rydell muses. "It was on the start-finish straight and there were the
three of us. One — I can't remember who — didn't see the third car.

Right *The podium at Trois Rivieres* (Bernard Brault/Canapress).

90

In fact I saw a picture of it in a Japanese motoring magazine and it was the one in the middle who moved over, that's how it began. Then the wheels banged and Jacques spun off in the middle of the straight. I think it was Tetsuya who hit him but I can't be sure."

Hiroshi Fushida worked for TOM's and was involved in both Formula 3 and Group C sportscars. "I met Jacques from the early part of the season and at that time he was very much a young boy. He's changed a lot since. He didn't look like a professional racing driver, just a young boy! Sometimes he was quiet, sometimes he spoke a lot — a very good young boy! He was not a gentleman, you understand. By that I mean not yet a real sophisticated gentleman. He was a young boy with talent. Yes, we could see the talent. In the beginning he didn't show the speed but once he got used to it he became quick and also very consistent. I think he still holds the record for finishing in the points in every championship race and there were a lot of good drivers, Rydell and other guys. It was one of the toughest years.

"At the end of the season, we were looking for a driver in Group C for the following year. We had good young drivers such as Kristensen, Irvine, Villeneuve, Rydell as well. We decided to give them a chance to drive a Group C car. It was not turbo but normally aspirated. For the last race of the Japanese Endurance series we tried Kristensen, Irvine and Villeneuve in one car. Our other car was driven by Geoff Lees and Jan Lammers [experienced ex-F1 drivers]. They won and the Villeneuve car came second.

"You could see the talent when he drove that Group C car, something he'd never driven before. He jumped into it and within 20 laps was showing a very good performance. Of course, because it was his first drive in such a car, we had to tell him *this* and *this* and *this* but I didn't need to tell him how to drive (chuckle). The brakes were completely different from what he'd known, carbon, and other things like that, but he adapted well."

Interestingly, Mauro Martini says that "after the Formula 3 Championship was over he tested a Formula 3000 car but I noticed that Jacques is the kind of driver who doesn't immediately go quick when he changes category. He's really methodical and that's why I was so impressed with him when he tested the Williams in 1995. I'm sure he didn't show his full potential and he'll get better. The guy doesn't want to have any accidents, for sure. He is the kind who firstly wants to know everything and secondly he's completely different from his father: he does not want any accidents *at all*. He knows his limits."

Of equal interest, Villeneuve contested a round of the Formula Atlantic series in August. He drove for a team called Comprep, which was backed by Player's — the tobacco company is a major motorsport sponsor — and finished third at Trois Rivieres. "Player's invited me to race in Canada," Villeneuve says. The reasons are so obvious they scarcely need elaboration.

After Villeneuve left the Formula 2000 school Richard Spenard lost track of him until he did the Atlantic race. "I was really impressed by the way he handled the whole weekend. He took his time, he did his work extremely systematically. He didn't feel the need to go fast immediately, he worked his way towards that. By the time the meeting had finished he was one of the fastest guys in Atlantic that weekend and there was fairly stiff competition.

"What impressed me also was the way he'd progressed since I'd known him. I didn't expect too much of him and he definitely

Testing the Team Comprep car, August 1992 (Michel Gravel/Canapress).

opened my eyes. He did *intelligently* well, adopted a very thoughtful approach to it. I said 'hello,' nothing special. He is not the warmest kid around, you know. You have to make an effort to be able to speak to him."

One spectator at Trois Rivieres was a Quebecois called Claude Bourbonnais, who had briefly and informally met Villeneuve at a kart track years before. "I hadn't seen him drive until he came over and did that one Atlantic race in 1992. Jacques adapts pretty well, he concentrates on what he has to do and he doesn't let too much around bother him. He treats it very much like a business."

Mauro Martini remembers that "he had a good season with TOM's in Japanese Formula 3 and finished every race in the points except one — the non-championship race at Suzuka. It wasn't his mistake, anyway. He was pushed off by another driver. That apart, Jacques was extremely consistent."

Magnanimous too. "When he left Japan, he didn't care about abandoning all the stuff in his flat. He called me and Mika Salo and the other guys and said 'hey, go into my flat and take whatever you want! I have to leave, I can't carry everything with me so just go in there and help yourselves . . .'"

To round the season off Villeneuve competed in the Macau Formula 3 Grand Prix. Reportedly, on the flight from Tokyo, Rydell fancied the window seat and grabbed it although Villeneuve ought to have had it — his boarding pass said so. Rydell wouldn't budge however much the "disgruntled" Canadian "cajoled" him. Meanwhile Kristensen grabbed the aisle seat leaving Villeneuve sandwiched between them. "What happened?" Rydell muses. "We were (chuckle) playing games like this the whole year. It was not to be unkind or anything, it was more like just a game that we took the best seats and he had to take the one that was left. Of course the stewardess wasn't very happy when he was still standing up and we were about to take off, so in the end he had to sit down! Probably he was angry at the time but then, of course, it was just a good laugh."

At Macau, Villeneuve was pitched in among a generation of ambitious hopefuls: not just Rydell, Kristensen and Reid but Lamy, Rubens Barrichello and Coulthard. Villeneuve qualified fifth, circling

Right *Talking about it, 1993* (Robert Nadon/Canapress).

Two minutes to go? Villeneuve in Formula Atlantic, 1993 (Robert Laberge/Canapress).

for a while with Colciago and Rydell. What ought to have been Villeneuve's hot lap perished when Colciago slowed and Rydell, evidently angry about that, got in front and gave Colciago the chop. Villeneuve found a way past them both but the time taken to achieve that negated everything. The race was run over two 15-lap heats and, in the first of them, Villeneuve took a trouble-free third place; in the second, Colciago moved swiftly away over the initial laps but Villeneuve caught and passed Kristensen. It made him third; and third overall.

Reflecting on Japan, Rydell says he — Rydell — "didn't have a problem with the Japanese because I tried to find out how they think. Of course it was difficult sometimes but I judge it to be not that bad. Sometimes, too, I miss the way we were living out there, the way we socialised between drivers, I miss that side of it but for sure I am very, very happy to be racing in England [in touring cars in 1995], I don't want to go back to Japan because it's just too far from home and so different. They obviously wanted Japanese drivers to win but they needed the Europeans for the sponsors and the credibility of the series. The team I drove for, of course they wanted me to win but if there was a team with one Japanese and one European driver I'd think — I don't say I'm sure — that they would want the Japanese to win.

"There is a problem with language. To say the same thing, they won't use the same words. They say it in a different way. The *yes* sometimes can be *no*. It's a terrible thing for them to say no so they will say yes — as if they understand the question but they'd really like to say no. You have to realise that. If you don't you have a big problem. Quite a lot of European drivers, or quite a lot of European people, I feel, are very direct and if it's a yes it's a yes."

Do you think Jacques had that problem?

"A little bit, for sure, because he was quite — well, what should I say? — a bit childish, although in a good way. Maybe he wouldn't understand what was happening on occasions, because he was still quite young compared to myself."

Did he strike you as intelligent?

"Yes. Jacques sometimes pretended not to understand and not to be too intelligent but he *knew* always. He was more intelligent than he made out to be." And as an aside, Rydell added: "Don't go writing bad things about Jacques. He's a good guy, a really good guy." I

The team of '93: Gerry Forsythe, Villeneuve, Claude Bourbonnais, Barry Green (Michel Gravel/Canapress).

haven't, Rickard, I haven't, and it's not self-imposed censorship. I haven't found anything bad to write.

Ruminating much later Villeneuve said: "As soon as I started racing in Italy at age 17 I was under tremendous pressure. I had to get mature quickly. If not I wouldn't have lasted very long. I also think that growing up and going to school in Switzerland, living in France, then racing three years in Italy and one in Japan I got to know many diverse cultures, and that's enabled me to adapt quickly to new situations.

"In a way, I kind of jumped over the last few years of my teens because of my career. I was racing instead of going to university and sometimes, you know, I'll watch movies or talk to people about university life and think 'that could have been fun!' On the other hand, I don't think that experience would have made me mature, but I'm perhaps more mature at my work than I am away from the track. At the end of a race weekend I like to get away and not think about racing. I like to listen to music, read fantasy books like Tolkien and play computer games. If it weren't for that, I'd get stressed-out by the next race weekend."

With girlfriend Sandrine Gros d'Aillon and manager Craig Pollock (Robert Laberge/ Canapress).

Mum seems pleased enough in 1993 (Robert Laberge/Canapress).

Villeneuve now decided to make a major move. He'd contest the 1993 Formula Atlantic season with a team to be called Forsythe-Green, partnering Bourbonnais. Barry Green, an Australian, had raced in Formula Ford and Formula 3 before moving to America, and had run four teams. Gerald Forsythe, a wealthy businessman, had been involved in racing since 1983.

"I'd made contact with Player's the year before that," Barry Green says, "with a view to them sponsoring me. How they finished up with Jacques as a guest driver for the Trois Rivieres race I don't know, but they had him over for it and they liked him. They thought if it could be a success it would be worth getting involved with him so they came back to me and we sat down with the three parties: Jacques' manager Craig Pollock, Player's and myself. We all liked what we were all saying and we all basically said 'well, if you do it I'll do it!'

"We drew up a three-year plan of how we'd go about it and that plan ran perfectly. Better than perfectly, really. The plan was one year in Formula Atlantic, IndyCar testing, IndyCar second and third years, but I'd have to stand up and say Jacques Villeneuve was ready for IndyCar the next year [1994], so there was a condition. I certainly wasn't going to put the guy in an IndyCar unless I thought he was ready. IndyCars, like Formula 1, are hard and fast and very dangerous.

"At that point Forsythe-Green didn't exist. I'd been on the road for several years trying to find a major sponsor to help set up my own team. I found Player's through a friend of mine, Rob Tanner, who had worked with them back in the 1970s when they were sponsoring the Formula Atlantic series in which Gilles ran. Anyway, I didn't think I had enough money [even with Player's] and I needed some help. That's when I went to Gerry Forsythe and asked him to join forces. The team was formed at the end of 1992."

Villeneuve would work with Tony Cicale, a very experienced race engineer who had worked with many big names including Mario Andretti. Cicale, who had not met Villeneuve before, quickly realised that he was "like a sponge. He soaked information up. You'd explain something very complicated to him and he'd understand immediately. I think the key is his intelligence." From all this something mighty would be forged.

Bourbonnais, who'd started in karts in 1983, had met Villeneuve once or twice as a kid. "There's a little kart track near Montreal called St-Hilaire. He must have been 12 or 13 and he was there with his uncle. I started to drive around with them — just rental karts, four-stroke five horsepower, although the owner did give us racing karts. You know, five horsepower only goes 50, 60 miles an hour but it was wet, we were on slicks and that was fun."

What sort of an impression did he make on you?

"Well, what can I say? It's pretty vague. He was just having fun."

Bourbonnais had won the Canadian Kart Championship and moved on to Formula 2000, came to Britain and did three Formula 2 races. "I ran out of money, returned home and did a couple of Atlantic races and that was it. By the end of 1992 I was travelling to the races to keep in touch and the Player's people happened to be there. This one guy, Vice President of the company, decided he was going to do something for me. We'd had a chat and I didn't know who he was. He asked me what I was doing at the race and I said I was trying to get a ride for next year. He knew what was going on for 1993 and decided that if the Villeneuve deal was going to happen there would be one more car for me."

If he had a bad day it didn't bother him — he had many different interests

---

Bourbonnais describes the Formula Atlantic cars as "very nice. I guess the tub would be similar to Formula 3. The power would be around 240 horsepower, four cylinders, and the cars have ground effects. They are as light as Formula 3s. The tyres are as wide as those in IndyCars or Formula 1 so that, while there's not much power, you do have a lot of grip. I liked a lot of G-loading in the corners because it suited my style of driving. I could really drive it hard."

Cicale "set myself to teach Jacques racing rather than just be his engineer, something I'd never done before because I'd been working with older, more experienced drivers. What impressed me was that if he'd had a bad day it didn't bother him. He had many different interests, like computer programming, and he wasn't one of those people who talk about and think about motor racing the whole time. It was unusual in a man of that age. He'd say *well, I do have other things in my life*. We built our relationship on trust. He never felt the need to impress anyone. He could be cold in the sense that he could put things completely out of his mind if he needed to."

Bourbonnais estimates that "it was quite a good team and I was very, very happy to be on board. The thing was to prepare Jacques to go IndyCar racing the following year."

Was that evident?

"Well, yes and no. I wasn't told that but I could feel it. Jacques and Tony Cicale formed a close relationship. Jacques worked with Tony and I didn't have an engineer. I had access to Tony between sessions. There was a guy on my car but he was a computer man, just writing down whatever I'd tell him. After a session I'd go talk to Tony and do whatever we had to do but during the session I didn't have an engineer."

That must have given you an indication of which way things were going.

"Oh, definitely. I knew exactly how things were going but some people very high in the company [Player's] that I trusted very much were telling me that it wasn't decided, and in their minds it wasn't, but . . ."

Cicale responds to the one-engineer situation. "Well, I'd say that's probably Claude's perspective and it's not totally accurate. Claude had an engineer who was my assistant at Team Green last year [1995], name of Scott Graves, very, very bright mechanical engineer. He was an inexperienced race engineer, he had no experience previous to that but he'd done a lot of mechanical drawing and been involved with teams for many years. Claude didn't feel he was as experienced, I guess, as he would have liked. I think in some ways Claude used that negatively."

To my question *was the weight of the team thrown behind Jacques?* Green responds "no, absolutely not. We had the three-year plan. That plan was in place, the contracts were signed and then Claude met the Player's people and they decided he would be a good asset to the team. So they came back to me and said 'can we run two cars?' I said 'yes, with this, this and this' and they said 'OK, let's do it.' Then I met Claude. The whole team was already set up to run Villeneuve and everything was in place to do that. Now we had another person, at which time we went out and got the very best people for the other person. Clearly Claude had everything that Jacques had, except Claude was Claude and Jacques was Jacques."

The 1993 Formula Atlantic season:

Round 1, Phoenix. Villeneuve crashed two cars comprehensively — the worse one being when he went off on oil in the morning warm-up and struck the wall. Repairs were attempted but he started from the back row in the spare.

Round 2, Long Beach. Villeneuve, pole, made a poor start, charged but needed four laps to overhaul a driver called Jamie Galles. Then he moved on Bourbonnais. Traffic caused them both problems and, on the last lap, Villeneuve collided with a back-marker. He limped home second despite a damaged wing.

Round 3, Road Atlanta. Gilles Villeneuve had won here twice in 1976, as so many people pointed out. Jacques took pole but after a melee at the start Bourbonnais led, Villeneuve following. Bourbonnais, however, spun off and, despite a strong challenge from a driver called Colin Trueman, Villeneuve was not to be caught. (Bourbonnais describes Trueman thus: "Colin's been in Atlantic since 1988, his mum owns the Mid Ohio circuit and he does it just for fun. He's worth a few million.")

Villeneuve said "winning your first race in any series is always very important. Until you have that first win you never know if it is really possible. The hairpin was breaking up real bad and our tyres picked up a lot of rubber while we were behind the pace car [after a crash] but other than that I had no problems."

Round 4, Milwaukee. A Texan called Greg Ray took pole but Villeneuve hounded him. On lap 11 Ray spun trying to lap a slower car and Villeneuve was too close to avoid contact with him. Exit both.

Round 5, Montreal. By now a formal announcement had been made that Villeneuve and the Forsythe-Green team would move up into IndyCars in 1994. Bourbonnais wouldn't be going with them. Of the race, *Motoring News* reported: "Villeneuve drove in a manner decidedly reminiscent of his parent on Saturday, when his electric dice with David Empringham kept observers on their toes throughout the 26-lap Atlantic clash. After losing the lead to Empringham, Villeneuve kept in touch and then grabbed back the initiative in the closing stages before going on to an emotional victory watched by his

Right *Victory in Montreal, 12 June, 1993* (Bernard Brault/Canapress).

mother and grandmother. It was highly appropriate that he should win impressively on the circuit named after his father." Here it was again, The Name and the comparison. (Bourbonnais describes Empringham thus: "A good driver, steady, very consistent. He was careful to finish all the races.")

Round 6, Mosport. Bourbonnais took pole and gained a second a lap over Villeneuve to beat him by 11 seconds. Empringham chased Villeneuve lustily but posed no real threat. Empringham now had 81 championship points, Bourbonnais and Villeneuve 74.

Round 7, Halifax. A tumult of a meeting. Bourbonnais crashed three times before the race and didn't start; Villeneuve crashed twice before the race and did start. He ran third towards the end, despite the fact that he'd gone off the circuit again; but the differential failed.

Round 8, Toronto. Bourbonnais led from beginning to end although, as the race unfolded, he suffered burns because fuel was seeping into the cockpit from a leak. Villeneuve joined battle with Empringham for second place until his fuel ran low in the closing laps.

Round 9, New Hampshire. Villeneuve took pole and led but Bourbonnais, determined, fashioned a decisive overtaking move on lap four to seize the lead for himself. Bourbonnais moved away, leaving Villeneuve and a driver called Mike Palumbo to wrestle over second place. Villeneuve held that and cut the gap to Bourbonnais to two seconds by the end.

Green ruminates on the background. "Shall we say that at the start of the season Claude and Jacques were good friends and then Claude, feeling that he was not getting everything that Jacques was, the friendship separated a little bit. They went off in their own directions. But let me tell you that the best thing to happen in Jacques' career was us hiring Claude Bourbonnais — because Claude was in his fifth or sixth or seventh year, I can't remember, but he was a very experienced Atlantic car driver. Jacques Villeneuve was not.

"Claude started out by kicking Jacques' butt, not so much in qualifying. Jacques we realised had a tremendous feel for the car and really helped us with set-ups, we used all his set-ups, he was brilliant at that. Jacques would always qualify well but, come race day, Claude just out-raced him. When the flag dropped, Claude took off and Claude was a heck of a racer. By half way through the season this started getting at Jacques, that Claude could actually beat him on race day; so Jacques had to reach down deep and take his driving to another level. By the end of the season it was clear that Jacques had improved his driving on race day tremendously and he proved he could out-qualify and out-race Claude Bourbonnais. If Claude hadn't been there it may have taken another year or two to get Jacques to the same level."

Round 10, Trois Rivieres. Jacques (Snr) was also competing in this, his 'home' event. "A wild race started with the three main championship contendors — Empringham, Bourbonnais and Villeneuve (Jnr) — sliding off at the first turn. All three resumed but Empringham was last," reported *Motoring News*. On lap 17 Villeneuve and Bourbonnais, coming up through the field, "clashed on the last corner and were forced to retire." Villeneuve (Snr) at one point led, but finished second to Empringham!

Jacques and Claude were very competitive,
but we would not tolerate any conflict

Bourbonnais says "it was all right during the year to have Jacques as a team-mate. He's pretty easy to get along with. We had one hard week-end, that was at Trois Rivieres and the *suchi* hit the fan. On the start the three of us went straight on at the first corner and the whole field went through. We were at the back and coming up fast, then there was a yellow flag so we could catch up. We began to pass people.

"I'd got Empringham behind, Jacques in front. I was catching him but he was baulking me a little bit. Coming out of the hairpin there's a very, very short straight [then a corner]. One lap Jacques was a little slower and I was a bit faster coming out. I wasn't prepared to try and pass him there. I was going to tuck in behind and brake but there wasn't time to brake. I was right on his gearbox so I made a move. I knew I had to be side-by-side on the braking to make sure I could turn in before him and that's what I did, but he turned into me. We banged wheels and were both out of the race.

"Trois Rivieres is a kind of Villeneuve fortress because they come from about 30 miles from there. It's a Villeneuve place — and

This is how he won Montreal. He leads David Empringham (Bernard Brault/Canapress).

Jacques, the uncle, was in the race too, leading for a while. Everyone was blaming me for the accident on the spot. Jacques was blaming me, too, and I was blaming him (chuckle). The next day people started to look at the video tapes and they kinda realised, hey maybe it's Jacques' fault. Our relationship recovered towards the end of the season. It was a little competitive from then on but we were still friends."

Cicale gives this insight: "I think the friction existed right from the very beginning of the season. Claude and Jacques were very competitive with each other: Claude wanted to beat Jacques and Jacques wanted to beat Claude, and it re-emphasised itself after Trois Rivieres. The friction is very, very, normal, oh absolutely, and it really didn't disrupt the team because we did not allow it to. Fortunately both drivers were on their way up, so to speak, and I was quite experienced and Barry was quite experienced. We would not tolerate any conflict amongst the team and it was as simple as that.

"They had their words among themselves, but from the engineering side and, I think, from the ownership side we just did not let it affect us. That's the problem with two-car teams. Once you get the personalities, once you get the people that have the strength and the control — which, of course, the Mario Andrettis, the Michael Andrettis, the Emerson Fittipaldis and the same type of individuals in Formula 1 have — once they get a reputation and garnish (exploit) the control of the team, trying to handle *that* is very, very difficult.

"Fortunately for us, both Claude and Jacques were not that big at the time so we'd say to them 'siddown, forget your differences, we're here working on the cars, we're going to try and do the best job we can, so Claude, forget your problems with Jacques and Jacques, forget your problems with Claude. Just let's get on with it.' I don't think it affected the team in much of a way at all." The conflict spurred each on to be yet more competitive, "which in some ways was quite good."

Round 11, Vancouver. Villeneuve, fifth on lap 8, dropped out when his halfshaft failed.

Round 12, Mid Ohio. Villeneuve took pole. Cicale says "Jacques went out and did a time faster than anybody else by about half a second. He came in and asked 'is that OK?' I said 'well, conditions

Podium, Mosport. Bourbonnais is centre, Empringham on the right (Graham Jardine/Canapress).

are improving, people will be running with lighter fuel loads and I think we need to find another second.' He went out again, went a second quicker and asked 'is that OK?' It was an amazing ability he had, one that I have not seen before."

He won the race "in the style of his Formula Atlantic double-champion father, Gilles" (*Autosport*). In taking pole, Villeneuve broke the track record by 0.2 of a second. Bourbonnais led by making a powerful start but Villeneuve charged and overtook him on lap 21. Bourbonnais said "there was a back-marker on the back straight. I was drafting him but Jacques got a draft off both of us. We both hit the brakes hard but he had the inside line for the next right-hander."

It was incredible what this kid could do once he had made up his mind

---

Reflecting, Bourbonnais says "I could have blocked him but I was generous there because of what happened in Trois Rivieres. Everyone was watching me. It was as if Villeneuve was — how can I say this? — the one everybody wanted to see winning. After Trois Rivieres it was hard, yes. It's an unwritten thing. You just feel it. Everyone talks to you about an incident like that and the main thing at Mid Ohio was not to take each other out. It seemed like it was all up to me [to make sure they didn't take each other out]."

Round 13, Nazareth. Bourbonnais took pole and won. Villeneuve, meanwhile, crashed in the second turn with a driver called Bobby Carville and pitted for repairs. It cost him four laps. He emerged with nothing to lose and broke the track record.

Round 14, Laguna Seca. Two races on successive days and Villeneuve won them both, as he needed to do to have any hope of the championship. Handily, he also took pole in both, each of them worth a point. In the first race, Villeneuve was "pressured every inch of the way" (*Autosport*). He and Bourbonnais "left the rest of the field well behind. Bourbonnais was relentless in his pursuit, yet Villeneuve was up to the task. He never so much as put a wheel wrong.Villeneuve always seemed to have a slight margin. A couple of times Bourbonnais took advantage of slower traffic to close up on the leader's tail, only for Villeneuve to turn in a couple of quick laps and re-establish his margin." Significantly, Empringham finished third.

Round 15, Laguna Seca. This was the championship-decider and all Bourbonnais needed was to finish *near* Empringham. And Empringham had crashed during qualifying, his time worth no more than eighteenth place. Villeneuve led with Bourbonnais travelling prudently behind him, Empringham roaring up the field. On lap 12 (of the 28) the engine in Bourbonnais' Ralt expired. Now a driver called Patrick LeMaire tracked Villeneuve but couldn't quite catch him while Empringham roared to fourth. It was enough. "I'm a lucky guy," he said. Empringham 195, Bourbonnais 191, Villeneuve 186.

I point out to Bourbonnais that Villeneuve's move to IndyCars had been announced at Montreal. "Hmmm, well, not in my book (chuckle). I mean, it was decided but they didn't tell me and it was just rumours in the newspapers. I found out the day of the last race at Laguna Seca. It was a weird situation. Some people from the company had promised Jacques the Indy ride but some other people in the company wanted me to have the ride. Oh, let me remember who told me. I can't even remember. It was put to me that Forsythe-Green would go to IndyCar with Jacques but not with me. I took it (sigh) . . . it was hard, you know. You beat the guy and then they tell you that he's getting the ride. That didn't affect our relationship, no it didn't." (Bourbonnais gives an evaluation of Villeneuve as a driver: "He's the opposite of his father. He likes to adjust the car a lot and not overdrive it but make it work for him, yep.")

Green says that "Claude kept claiming he was never told that the deal was in place with Villeneuve for the future. I personally sat down with Claude three times over the season at dinner, one-on-one, just the two of us, and told him what the situation was."

A happier postscript. Cicale says that he and Villeneuve "became so close that I decided to stay in motor racing. On the last day of the Atlantic series I said 'he will win the Indy 500, he will win the IndyCar Championship and he will become Formula 1 World Champion.' *That* is the sort of ability he had."

Green says that "looking back and reviewing the season, it was incredible what this kid Jacques Villeneuve could do once he had made up his mind. He decided 'I've had enough of this, I'm going to beat that guy [Bourbonnais].' He got focused and away he went."

• CHAPTER FOUR •

Rub
of the Green

INDYCAR IS THE only rival to Formula 1 in the world — IndyCar people insist the comparison should be the other way round. As well as inherent differences there are many similarities: 16 or 17 races per season on a variety of circuits, big names, journeymen, ambitious youngsters, and overall the same mentality. There's a cross-fertilisation between the two but generally from Formula 1 to the United States, not the other way round.

The inherent differences: IndyCars are constructed to quite separate rules, they have turbos, some of the races are on oval circuits, and the races have many more 'go-slows' behind pace cars if anything goes wrong, like crashes. IndyCar tactics are therefore much more subtle and fluid. Racers bunch behind a pace car, so you may have several rolling re-starts during a race as the pace car releases them; and many laps behind a pace car saves fuel, altering the pit stop strategy and the whole race.

This chapter includes some explanations about the mechanisms of certain situations for non-followers of IndyCar, so I ask the patience of North American readers and those elsewhere who are familiar with the sport. I'm indebted to Gordon Kirby of *Autosport* and Bob Walters, the Director of Public Relations at Indianapolis, for help.

IndyCars are fearsomely swift on ovals. At the Indianapolis 500 in

1994, Emerson Fittipaldi, once of Formula 1 of course, *averaged* 230.438mph on his hottest lap. A Formula 1 car reaches around 210mph — at a place like Hockenheim — but not more, because of the nature of the circuits.

The IndyCar scoring is: 20, 16, 14, 12, 10, 8, 6, 5, 4, 3, 2, 1 with 1 for pole, 1 for most laps led.

This initial thumb-nail sketch is designed to explain how daunting it can be for the rookie — the first-year man — to go IndyCar racing and thus provide a context for what Villeneuve would do. Apart from Fittipaldi the big names he'd face included fellow Canadian Paul Tracy and Al Unser Jnr (all three in the Penske team, who made their own cars and would be dominant), Nigel Mansell and Mario Andretti (Newman-Haas/Lola), Michael Andretti (Ganassi/Reynard) and Robby Gordon (Walker/Lola). Other drivers would cut across his path, some literally.

Now another context. Pete Spence worked for Cosworth, who supplied Marlboro McLaren with engines in 1993 — Ayrton Senna's last year with the team before moving to Williams — and the Green

Into IndyCar 1994 (Robert Laberge/Canapress).

Reynard which Villeneuve drove in 1994 and 1995. He is arguably the best placed man on earth to evaluate the current comparisons being made between Senna and Villeneuve. Spence feels the comparison is valid.

"I have to say there are similarities in the level of commitment. The thing you notice is how aware they are, how observant they are. You could be sitting in the motorhome de-briefing with Ayrton after a morning session, trying to pick a set-up for the car for the afternoon qualifying. He'd gaze outside, he'd notice the flags on poles and say 'look, the wind has changed' or maybe 'the sun has come out so the track temperature will be greater.' He noticed all these things. Unless you're *really* switched on, you don't think about them. There are so many drivers who just get in the car and drive."

Like Gilles, in fact?

"Yes."

How does it apply to Jacques? Was he the same as Senna?

"I'd say he was. I had a very interesting conversation with Tony Cicale at the IndyCar banquet this year (1995). Tony Cicale is a very clever engineer and also a keen wind-surfer. He said, corny as it may sound, that setting his windsurfer up for different wind conditions — at the level at which he competes — taught him a great deal. It wasn't necessarily because of dynamic similarities between cars and windsurfs that taught him, it was how to respond to minor changes and set up for them; and that applied to a car.

"To make a car perform to its optimum, you cannot assume that because the car was good in the first session it will be the same in the second session. You have to watch all the factors which affect the car, weather, track, tyre conditions. This approach helped him to understand how best to set the car up. Listening to Villeneuve, he's like that. You can hear the level of his awareness and it is similar to Ayrton although, perhaps, without the wealth of experience that Ayrton had.

"These people work like human data loggers. The first time we ran a Ford HB engine with Ayrton at Silverstone he spun off after a couple of laps: the torque delivery of the V8 was so different to the V12 he'd been used to [McLaren ran a Honda V12 before the Japanese withdrew at the end of 1992]. He went out again and did an installation lap and then he did 10 laps in a row. He came in after

114

With Tony Cicale after Villeneuve had passed the rookie test at Indianapolis
(Michael Conroy/Canapress).

those 10 laps and recounted each one, recounted each corner of each
lap like you were strolling through a data log. It was amazing. He'd
say 'on the third lap — or maybe it was the fourth, no it was the third
— I clipped a kerb on the inside.' These were minor things most
people just would not remember. Jacques could do that too.

"Engine-wise, the feed-back which Jacques gave was very good and
it's always useful as an engine man to be corrected by the driver.
Often drivers will say things to you and you'll think *hmm, well, I don't
honestly believe you because if something like that had happened the engine*

115

would have failed completely. Or perhaps there is no real reason — if the engine is in good condition — for it to lose power by the amount that you feel it has.

"Drivers say these things and, when you dyno-test the engine afterwards, the dyno does not bear that out. Now with Jacques, and with Ayrton, what they said was accurate. There were times when we had problems with our gear shift electronics system. If Jacques told you something had happened in a particular sequence and you challenged him he'd pick you up on that and say 'it's as I said. This happened first . . .'

"That's good because if they are sufficiently aware they can recount a sequence of events — or systems — in chronological order, no matter that they took place in the space of a gear shift, which is a tenth of a second or less. It points to good mechanical understanding."

Also it is a gift to be able to do it.

"Yeah, I agree absolutely. Such drivers are just like computers. They appear to have a much higher processing speed. They're like this: you're walking along as fast as you can and they walk up behind and trip you. Their whole lives, their whole existence, moves at an accelerated speed."

So Forsythe-Green went to IndyCars. "In the first year," Cicale says, "I made sure Jacques had plenty of time to get up to his maximum, say 10 laps or whatever he needed. However in the second year we realised that that wasn't good enough and you had to be up to speed much quicker. We talked it over, he listened and that's what he did."

Green says that "at our last IndyCar test we sat down and I had three pages of notes. Jacques and I went over them at dinner one night. It was like an exam: he was asking me questions and I'd ask him questions. I told him that his biggest problem would be finishing the first three races, and I wasn't wrong, but before the season started we tried to *re-live* all the problems he was going to have. Not only I did that, but Tony would do that too. Not too many people have gone into IndyCar with the same opportunity that Jacques had with us, to cover the miles in testing. That was all in the plan, and that was all because Player's agreed to the plan and sponsored it."

The IndyCar career began at Surfers' Paradise, Queensland, on 20 March 1994. Villeneuve qualified on the fourth row of the grid, riding the kerbs with intent. In the race he was running fifth towards the end when he collided with Stefan Johansson (Bettenhausen/Penske) which sent him into the wall.

At Phoenix he put the car on the front row. David Phillips in *Motoring News* wrote that Villeneuve "used his early draw in the qualifying order together with a nearly perfect set-up on the Player's Reynard-Cosworth (the legacy of more than 1,000 miles of winter testing at Phoenix and the expertise of Forsythe-Green engineer Tony Cicale) to shatter the existing lap record with a 20.442s — and give himself a nice twenty-third birthday present into the bargain. 'I had a little understeer that last lap in Turn Four,' he said. 'And the pop-off valve blew open on my best lap so I had to lift a little.' Nobody else even got close to that time until Tracy uncorked a 20.424 to secure the pole."

> *The press said he was wild, like his father, but there was no comparison, as drivers or men*

The race was controversial and I make no excuse for quoting extensively two contemporary reports, even though they overlap. Phillips wrote that on lap 62 "running thirteenth after stopping under the yellow (yellow lights or flags, following an accident), Teo Fabi [Hall/Reynard] tried to go around the high side of Hiro Matsushita [Simon/Lola] in Turn Three and was most of the way past when the Lola's right nose wing clipped his left rear. Both cars cannoned into the Turn Four wall, taking the hapless Tracy with them even as Fittipaldi made it through. Several other cars passed before Villeneuve unaccountably stormed into Turn Three behind the slowing Mario Andretti and Arie Luyendyk [Indy Regency/Lola]. The Canadian moved up high and rammed Matsushita's stricken machine amidships. Observers said he only began to brake mere feet before the impact.

"Hiro's car all but exploded in a cloud of expensive pieces, the monocoque spinning topsy turvy into the infield — collecting the unfortunate Dominic Dobson [PacWest/Lola] in the process — even as the engine and transaxle went for a ride along the wall. Incredibly, Hiro escaped with nothing more than a separated shoulder while

Jacques was unscathed — physically. 'When the yellow came out, they came on the radio and I was already a little high and started braking because Luyendyk was there overtaking someone,' he said. 'There wasn't much room on the inside and I was braking a little bit on the outside. Then I saw the two cars that were stopped and I couldn't avoid them.'"

Gordon Kirby wrote in *Autosport* of a "wild multi-car accident. The accident was triggered by Matsushita clipping wheels with Fabi, as Fabi tried to lap the Japanese driver. The leaders were running directly behind this pair, and as Fabi and Matsushita's cars spun into the retaining wall, Tracy found himself with nowhere to go. He was taken into the wall by Matsushita's car, who was then hit amidships by Villeneuve. The young Canadian rookie's Reynard T-boned Matsushita's car, and was then in turn hit by Dobson. It was remarkable that Villeneuve escaped uninjured from his wrecked Reynard, which ended up partway down the pit lane. If nothing else, the accident certainly demonstrated the strength of the Reynard which was estimated to have taken a 20g impact in the shunt."

Villeneuve insisted he wasn't "driving crazy or anything." He'd defend himself in more detail later, as we shall hear.

Cicale offers interesting insights into this and Surfers' Paradise. "The couple of accidents were only very partially his fault and the other drivers and the press were saying 'he's wild like his father.' But he wasn't. There is no comparison between the two, as drivers or as men. With any team, including Formula 1, the question is how does the team respond when things aren't going your way. Is that trust still there? Has the driver surrounded himself with people that really do believe in him and will look after him?" Tony Cicale believed in Villeneuve and fully intended to look after him.

At Long Beach, where Bourbonnais made his debut for a team called Proformance Lola, Villeneuve qualified on the seventh row and was in a struggle with Marco Greco [Arciero/Lola], Fabi and Scott Goodyear [Budweiser King/Lola] before he spun into the tyres in Turn Seven. He was fifteenth, five laps behind the winner, Unser. Bourbonnais, incidentally, retired after 28 laps when the exhaust failed.

Right *A second place in the Indy 500 and he looks pleased, not delirious* (Tom Russo/Canapress).

118

"After Long Beach," Green recalls, "I said 'Jacques, remember that meeting when I said the problem would be finishing the first three races' and he said 'yeah.' I said 'I was right, wasn't I?' He listens. Again there, he listened. He'll say 'right, these are my problem areas' and he goes and works on them. Every time we picked a fault, two or three races down the road you could forget about it.

"There are always new challenges. The pit lane procedures in IndyCar are crucial, for example. We kept emphasising how important the pits were and we won a couple of races in the pits. He became the best guy in the pits. Again he set his mind to it but it was *we*, it was a whole *we* group. It wasn't just Jacques, it wasn't me, it wasn't Tony Cicale, it wasn't the crew, it was the group. It was one tremendous group effort."

Thus far Villeneuve had done nothing to suggest that he'd even get to the end of the Indianapolis 500, centre-piece of the IndyCar calendar and arguably the biggest motor race anywhere. Certainly in global terms only the Monaco Grand Prix and the Le Mans 24-hour sportscar race stand alongside it. All else aside, Indianapolis — taking practice, qualifying, and the race — lasts a month. It is a rack of an examination of everyone involved. In 1994 that was from Saturday 7 May to Sunday 29 May.

The meeting began beneath a long shadow. On Saturday 30 April in the San Marino Grand Prix at Imola, Roland Ratzenberger, driving a Simtek Ford, died in the practice session. It was the first death at a Grand Prix meeting for 12 years. The next day Ayrton Senna died in hospital after crashing at Tamburello driving a Williams. This produced global grief. At another level Senna's death was to alter the whole power balance in Formula 1 for years to come. His death would exercise a direct bearing on the career of Jacques Villeneuve.

How do you approach the Indy 500 with a rookie?

"Well," Cicale says, "the same way as we approached the entire season. We went there in the winter and did a number of laps with Jacques. Primarily what we tried to do with Jacques the first year was simply give him a reliable, basic car that he could count on, that he could trust. We really didn't push him to do anything in particular. We didn't say 'Jacques, go out and in five laps you have to do a certain speed.' We always made sure that he had the time to learn the car very slowly, bring it up to speed very slowly and of course with the

Win a
£25 BOOK TOKEN

As a sports book reader we are very interested in your views on this and other titles.

Please complete and return the questionnaire below and we will enter you into our quarterly draw to win one of two **£25 book tokens**.

Book Title

1 Do you consider this book good value for money ?

Very Good Value ▷☐   Good Value ▷☐   Not Good Value ▷☐   Poor Value ▷☐

2 Which of the following statements do you agree with about this book ?
(please tick all which apply)

There are too many pictures ▷☐   There are not enough pictures ▷☐

There are too many pages ▷☐   There are not enough pages ▷☐

The book should be hardback ▷☐   There should be more colour pictures ▷☐

The page size is too small ▷☐   The page size is too large ▷☐

3 Would you be prepared to pay for more colour photographs ?

No ▷☐   Yes, £1 more ▷☐   Yes, £2 more ▷☐   Yes, £5 more ▷☐

4 Which sports are you interested in reading about ?

Soccer ▷☐   Horse Racing ▷☐   Tennis ▷☐   Golf ▷☐   Cycling ▷☐

Cricket ▷☐   Rugby Union ▷☐   Rugby League ▷☐   Motorsport ▷☐

Other *(please list)*

5 Which other specific subjects/personalities would you be interested in reading about?

6 Where did you find out about this book ?

Magazine/Newspaper Review ▷☐   Bookshop ▷☐   Mail Order Catalogue ▷☐

Magazine advertisement ▷☐   It was a gift ▷☐

Other *(please specify)*

7 Where did you buy this book ?

Bookshop ▷☐   Mail Order ▷☐   Motor Accessory Shop ▷☐

Other *(please specify)*

Name

Address

Post Code

Home Telephone Number

Male ▷☐   Female ▷☐   Age: 15-24 ▷☐ 25-34 ▷☐ 35-44 ▷☐ 45-54 ▷☐ 55-64 ▷☐ 65+ ▷☐

If you do not wish to receive information on any other Haynes product or related service please tick this box ▷☐

Mario Andretti (left) presents Villeneuve with the Mario Andretti Award for rookie of the year, 1994 (Frank Gunn/ Canapress).

Uncle Jacques drove in the 1994 Formula Atlantic race at Trois Rivieres. Nephew Jacques giving **him** *advice?!?* (Bernard Brault/ Canapress).

Elkhart Lake, Villeneuve has just plundered a path past the Penskes and is poised to take his first IndyCar victory (David Boe/ Canapress).

experience that I had and the experience that Barry had we tried to eliminate a lot of the obvious loopholes — a lot of the problems that an inexperienced driver would normally have.

"But Jacques adapts to situations very, very well. He almost relishes a new situation, so in fact it wasn't really a huge problem for him. He listens very carefully, he does exactly what you tell him to do, he makes very few mistakes and he never drives beyond the limit of his or the car's ability. Consequently he never really got into trouble that first year. The first year in particular he took the Indy 500 in his stride."

Day One was rained off. By five in the afternoon of Day Two the rookies had passed what is called the final observation phase of their tests, Villeneuve among them. The test was a sequence of laps at differing speeds to demonstrate that the driver can control the car properly apart from wringing enormous speed from it. On Day Three Villeneuve was ninth (222.651mph against Michael Andretti, quickest, 227.038). On Day Four, the pace increasing, Villeneuve did 226.637 (against Raul Boesel, Dick Simon/Lola, 230.403). He didn't run on Day Five, did on Days Six and Seven but couldn't reach the top ten. It brought him to Pole Day, and here is a word of explanation.

There are in fact four qualifying days for positions on the grid (the first Saturday and Sunday, the second Saturday and Sunday) *but* the times are in descending scale of importance: a moderate time on the first Saturday beats a faster time on the first Sunday and so on down. It creates a proper shoot-out on that first Saturday, which Americans seem to like. That's why it's called Pole Day.

During the morning practice 25 drivers produced speeds they hadn't reached thus far, including Villeneuve at 227.066. At 1.12pm he moved out into serious qualification and put this sequence together

Seconds	Mph
39.768	226.313
39.637	227.061
39.798	226.142
39.907	225.524

Right *The victory, Elkhart Lake* (Todd Ponath/Canapress).

It represented fourth overall: 227.061 the most a rookie had ever done, the four-lap sequence the most a rookie had ever done too. "It feels great to be here," he said, predictably enough. "I did not expect to be this fast. I was flat out from the word go. At first I wasn't seeing enough boost, and I had to bring the gauge up but it was a good run."

He ran on Days Ten (third), Eleven (ninth), Fifteen (eleventh) and Seventeen (Carburetion Day) when he took part in the Miller Genuine Draft Pit Stop Championship — the Green team won, changing all four wheels and refuelling in 12.867 seconds, the second best time ever. "The team's been working hard all month. They gave 100% of themselves and I'm happy we could get that win." To the team it was worth $25,000.

There's a rich anecdote about one of these days, which Green recounted to Nigel Roebuck of *Autosport*. "The kid's feel for the race car, and his feedback to the engineers, is as good, if not better, than I've ever known — which is unbelievable when you think how little mileage he's had so far. He learns fast and he excels under pressure.

A stunning start to 1995. Villeneuve wins the opening race, Miami (Bill Tuttle/Canapress).

As well as that, he's calm. In fact he's so low-key when he's driving that we can't get him to talk loudly on the radio. We have to remind him all the time to speak up. He'd just done a lap at 224mph and then he said quietly 'I've had two wheels on the grass.' I looked at the other guys. 'What did he say, did I hear him right?'

"That lap was 223.7 and then he did a 225 and came in. I asked him about what he'd said on the radio, and it turned out he'd been coming up on Willy T Ribbs out of Turn Two. All of a sudden Willy decides he's going to come in — and Jacques is on a hot lap so the closing speed is tremendous. He's committed to going down low and passing Ribbs — and Willy doesn't see him. Jacques keeps going, puts two wheels on the grass, and the lap is still 223.7! When he told us there was no emotion whatsoever. He's a cool one."

And that was it until the Sunday and the race. The build-up is extrovert Americana writ large and enough to unsettle any young man when it is balanced against what he knows is coming next: 500 miles in just over three hours, 200 laps, a long way to go, and dangerous. Villeneuve approached it pragmatically. "I made a slow start, just took it easy." He didn't run with the leaders but led the following pack. "I had a lot of understeer at the beginning, then after half-tanks it went to oversteer. It was getting sideways on me everywhere. That wasn't nice."

[Half-tanks? Cicale explains that "there are a number of yellows that get thrown, particularly during the oval races. As a general rule of thumb, if you have less than half fuel load you'll come in and take on fuel if there is a yellow. And 75 to 80% of the time that's probably the right strategy. Given a normal situation, you will stop under the yellow if you have half a fuel load or less".]

Villeneuve stalled at his first pit stop and lost eight places. "I was really mad after that, but it's a long race." He circled twelfth.

Phillips reported: "With little fanfare Jacques Villeneuve has stayed within striking distance, despite stalling on his first pit stop. Thanks to stop 'n' goes to Eddie Cheever [Menard/Lola] and Mansell as well as the trouble encountered by John and Michael Andretti [puncture/handling problems respectively] not to mention some determined driving, Jacques moved back to seventh by lap 50. Twelve laps later the Forsythe-Green entry took over the lead for a couple of tours, courtesy of good fuel mileage that enabled him to run

125

The pit stop strategy which helped Villeneuve regain two laps at Indianapolis (Tom Strattman/Canapress).

four to six laps more than the Penskes between stops. 'When my crew put "1" on my pit board I didn't know what they meant. Did that mean I was pitting in one lap? Then I looked at the big scoring tower and thought *huh, the Penskes must have gone in for fuel or something. I knew they would fly back past me.*'

At **62** Unser and Fittipaldi had made normal stops and Villeneuve became the first rookie to lead the Indianapolis 500 in 1994.

Would the Penskes fly back past?

"Well, yes and no," wrote Phillips. "Certainly the Penskes reclaimed the lead with ease once the Player's Reynard pitted, but when Jacques rejoined he found himself just a few lengths away from being lapped by Fittipaldi — who had lapped everyone else (save for Unser) by this stage; but the plucky French-Canadian would have none of that, and stayed clear of the Marlboro Merc for nearly 20 laps before succumbing."

At **68**: Fittipaldi led from Unser by 16.4 seconds and Villeneuve by 42.2. Only these three were on the lead lap.

On **74** Fittipaldi led by 14 seconds from Unser.

On **92** the field bunched under yellow — an accident. Mansell was travelling slowly and the car of Dennis Vitolo [Simon/Lola] rode up onto him. When all this was cleared, Villeneuve worked his way back onto the lead lap.

At **117** Fittipaldi led by 10.1 seconds from Unser and 28.1 from Villeneuve.

On **125** the Penskes pitted. Villeneuve led again.

At **128** Villeneuve led by 2.4 seconds from Fittipaldi, who reclaimed the lead two laps later when Villeneuve pitted.

At **152** Fittipaldi led by 31.4 seconds from Unser and 36.8 from Villeneuve. Five laps later Fittipaldi lapped Villeneuve.

"The final 50 laps," Phillips wrote, "boiled down to a three-way duel between Emmo, Al and Jacques. Fittipaldi clearly had the best car but Unser was lurking ready to take advantage of any bobble. Jacques still had a glimmer of a chance thanks to his fuel mileage that gave the Player's team some thought of trying to go the final 34 laps on a single stop while the Penskes would almost certainly have to make a regular stop plus a splash 'n' dash in the final five laps." Meanwhile Fittipaldi lapped Unser who promptly responded by unlapping himself.

On **185** Fittipaldi hit a kerb and then the wall. Out. By something of an irony, perhaps, the yellow after Fittipaldi's crash enabled Unser to run to the end without a stop, thus negating any Villeneuve fuel-economy advantage.

At **190** Unser led by 5.0 seconds from Villeneuve, but that would stretch through 15, 18 and 23 seconds to **195**. Unser did have one final moment on **197**. A driver called Stan Fox [Hemelgarn/Reynard] crashed and Unser had to tip-toe through the debris. The racers were held under yellow for the remaining three laps: nobody could overtake anybody. Villeneuve's time: 3 hours 06.37606 seconds.

I knew the team could win so I had to maintain my focus and do my job

---

"I never intended to catch Al. I didn't want to lose [my second place] because I think third was 25 seconds behind me. I just wanted to keep a little gap to the end. When I saw people fighting like crazy all around me I lifted and took it easy. It would have been stupid to end up in the wall at that point when all we had to do was finish. It's something I never dreamed of — being on the podium. I was hoping, but I never thought I could make it. I was very confident in the team though. I knew they were capable of winning so I had to maintain my focus and do my job."

The Question reared, as it would. About your father? "The only memories I have are of being a kid — the memories you have of your father, not a race car driver. He died when I was young and I didn't know anything about racing at that point anyway. Definitely I would be happy to see his face today if he was here. I think he would be proud. Indianapolis is the one place where you have to stay concentrated for a long period of time. Not only is it the longest race, it's a whole month from the start of practice to the end of the race. It's easy to lose your focus, to get mad if things aren't going well. But nothing happened to me . . . so maybe I wasn't out of my head! We spent the whole month without losing focus."

Villeneuve answered the criticism after Surfers' Paradise and Phoenix. "I'll be a rookie the whole season and if anything happens eyes will be on me if I'm in the middle of it. That always happens with rookies so I don't complain about it. A lot has happened this season in Australia and at Phoenix and I'm happy this has changed things a little bit."

(Bourbonnais, who wasn't in the race, says that although "the whole Forsythe-Green team was brand new to IndyCar, a lot of people in it had been IndyCar racing before." *How did you feel when Jacques came second?* "Well, I was a bit jealous. I wanted that ride . . .")

At Milwaukee, Villeneuve ran as high as fourth but the car felt loose and he was given a stop 'n' go for overtaking under yellow before the green flag. He finished ninth. After Milwaukee, Villeneuve amplified his defence. "What happened at Phoenix could have happened to anybody. Of course whatever happens is partly your fault because you're the one in the car, so in a way people were right to criticise me, but when they say I didn't see the yellow lights, I say I didn't see the yellow lights at Milwaukee either even though I

The historic and astonishing triumph at Indianapolis (Mark Matheny/Canapress).

was looking very hard for them. And at those speeds even if you see the yellow lights there's nothing you can do.

"People said I didn't put the brakes on until I was on top of the accident [in Phoenix] but I was on the brakes earlier. I was criticised for being crazy, driving out of my mind, but I was driving very comfortably, in control. Things like that happen to everybody once in a while. If you do great in 10 races then make one mistake, people remember the mistake, and the mistake is even more noticeable when you're a rookie."

At Detroit he ran prudently to seventh. At Portland he finished sixth, a lap adrift after "another impressive performance" (Kirby in *Autosport*). He'd stayed close to Mansell and Gordon early but lost time in traffic and, for a whole tract of the race, remained captive behind Adrian Fernandez [Galles/Reynard]. "He was quite fast down the straights and I couldn't overtake him. Most of the race I was stuck behind him and there was nothing I could do about it, but we finished well and got some more points. I'm not unhappy."

At bumpy Cleveland, an airport circuit (and from a Formula 1 standpoint an amazing place for a race, a bit like the original, raw, unshaped airbase called Silverstone) Villeneuve consolidated. He was fastest in the race morning warm-up and sixth as it unfolded, keeping an even pace. Fourth here made him seventh in the championship with 46 points.

It was a bare mid-season, as rookie mid-seasons are apt to be. The tide goes the other way and it's hard to say quite why, but it does. At Toronto he was ninth. At Michigan he didn't finish, accident. At Mid Ohio Michael Andretti had a "wild" race, banging wheels with several drivers, Villeneuve among them. He finished ninth.

New Hampshire was bizarre, to say the least. On this one-mile oval the cars came round on the rolling start — but, headed towards the green and in changing from first gear to second, Fernandez slewed sideways, creating mayhem. Villeneuve and Luyendyk ended up in the wall. At Vancouver the exhaust let go.

And thence to Elkhart Lake, Wisconsin, an almost pastoral circuit. He qualified on the front row alongside Tracy who led, Villeneuve harrying him, and Unser harrying Villeneuve — then a stall during his first pit stop cost Villeneuve the second place. He was third and that set up a sprint at the final re-start after the pace car pulled off.

Brimming with aggression he passed both Tracy and Unser into Turn One, three cars abreast. Villeneuve dived inside Tracy *as* Unser was outside. Tracy veered inside and clipped Villeneuve's rear wheel. "Paul hit me a little bit in the back. That knocked me sideways but I was able to get in to the corner ahead of them. I knew Paul could afford to make a mistake and go off [Tracy was out of contention for the championship] but Al couldn't. He had to finish the race. I knew he wouldn't try anything wild.

"I thought the corner would be the best chance for me to pass. I was quicker than them on the straights but I couldn't get close enough to pass because I'd lose downforce when I was behind. So I was going to go for it on the re-start. The fact that Paul made a mistake and got too close to the pace car helped me. He had to back off and that enabled me to get a tow."

Unser pursued Villeneuve to the end. "Jacques was awfully quick down the straight. What I was really trying to do was push him into a mistake but he drove a perfect race." Villeneuve one hour 44 minutes 40.88 seconds, Unser one hour 44 minutes 41.89.

Cicale describes Villeneuve as "outstanding" here. "We had decided quite early on — and this was our general strategy all along — that we'd run less downforce than a lot of the other teams. Jacques was willing to do that. Certainly most of your passing takes place under braking. In order to pass under braking, you have to be close at the end of the straightaway straight. We set up the car so our straightaway speeds would be higher. If we could maintain good consistent braking at the end of the straight nobody could pass him or he would have the ability to pass other people." At Wisconsin, it worked.

At the next race, Nazareth, Villeneuve finished seventh which confirmed him as Rookie of the Year — and, incidentally, now the great Mansell had only three points more: Mansell 83, Villeneuve 80. Reportedly the majority of drivers complained their cars were "tail-happy," especially in traffic, Villeneuve was one of them. Villeneuve had an encounter with Fernandez — they rubbed wheels when Fernandez essayed a "rather optimistic manoeuvre around the outside." Fernandez wasn't hurt. His car was.

Right *The traditional milk for the conqueror* (Al Behrman/Canapress).

It left Laguna Seca. There Mario Andretti made his final IndyCar appearance, ending an era spanning four decades and embracing both Formula 1 and IndyCar Championships. Villeneuve, maybe, was the dawn of a new era. Tracy was extremely robust here although Villeneuve ran with him early and, later, scythed past Fittipaldi, putting two wheels off onto the dirt but keeping absolute control of the car. *That* put you in mind of Gilles: just this once the intuitive bravura. Boesel took second place from him when he locked brakes in traffic.

Villeneuve spoke of how he'd approached the season, "hoping for a few top tens and maybe some podiums near the end of the year." As it was, he occupied sixth place in the Championship with 94 points, in front of Boesel (90) and Mansell (88). Villeneuve said he hadn't re-signed with Green yet but felt so close to the team that he expected to soon; and did.

The career which had begun such a short time ago — 1988 in Alfa Romeos — was accelerating.

Villeneuve took the new Team Green Reynard to the Sebring circuit in Florida just before Christmas. He shattered the lap record on day one and shattered it again on day three. "The car seems to be less sensitive and more driveable than the old one. I like it. It's fun and it seems to be quick." It would not be so easy or so smooth. In January 1995 he tested at Firebird's East and West road courses — on the East he covered 217 laps with a best of 43.9 seconds, half a second off the time he'd set the year before. What did that mean? You can never really tell until the cars roll onto the grid for the first race of a campaign which would last from Miami in March to Laguna Seca in September.

The 1995 IndyCar season:
Round 1, Miami. Villeneuve spoke of "problems" in winter testing and a less than satisfactory qualifying — eighth — here. He judged the car would be "strong" in the race but nursed no hopes of winning. Someone described the race round this street circuit — IndyCar hadn't been to the city for a generation — as requiring patience,

Right *In his own right now, all right. They want his autograph because of what he's become* (Robert Laberge/Canapress).

134

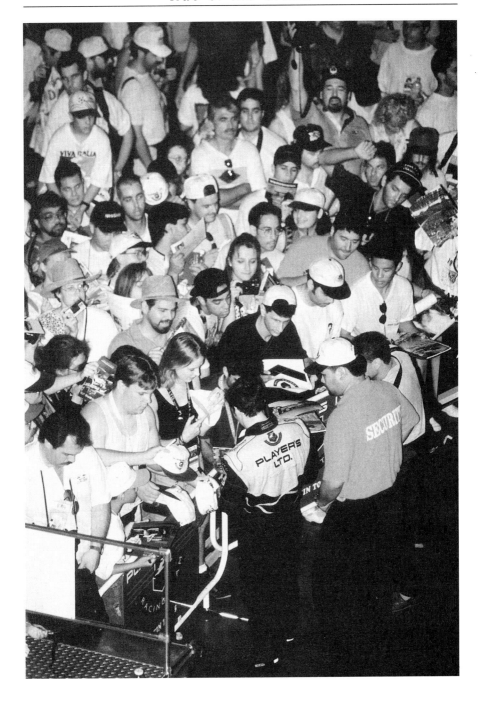

teamwork and survival, true of all races but especially here. Michael Andretti led, Villeneuve sixth but becoming fourth when Gil de Ferran (Hall/Reynard) had a gearbox failure and Christian Fittipaldi (Walker/Reynard) was given a stop 'n' go penalty for a pit lane infringement.

After the first pit stops Villeneuve emerged third. Andretti struck a wall, making him second to Mauricio Gugelmin (Ganassi/Reynard). The race turned on the next pit stops, from which Villeneuve emerged in the lead. Gugelmin said, "he was 200 yards down the road from me when I came out of the pits. There were no mistakes on my team so Jacques' must have done a superb stop." To which Villeneuve commented: "Our first pit stop was great but the second even better. I don't think we've had one as good." He thought *I can win it from here.* What he couldn't afford was any semblance of a mistake among the unforgiving walls as Gugelmin tracked him. He made no mistake. The post-race ebbed into controversy: Christian Fittipaldi claimed he'd had to pit on lap 19 because Villeneuve "hit me and punctured one of my tyres."

I really had to work hard to keep Jacques behind me, he did an incredible drive — Fittipaldi

---

"That's bull!" Villeneuve responded. "I didn't hit him at all. I don't know where he got that from. It's probably an excuse — they teach a lot of that in Formula 1. (Fittipaldi had just arrived from three seasons in Formula 1.) He was driving from side to side across the track from the first lap." Villeneuve, meanwhile, explained he'd had brake problems and it was extremely hot "but I guess that was the same for everyone."

It was.

Round 2, Surfers' Paradise. He qualified on the front row alongside Michael Andretti although not without a scramble: suspension problems, and a broken rear wishbone bolt only repaired with 10 minutes left. "That's when you go crazy. You use the kerbs and drive very aggressively. Sometimes it pays off and I guess it did today." In the race he ran second, was relegated to third and the transmission failed.

Round 3, Phoenix. A hectic race anticipated, the anticipation fulfilled. During it Villeneuve and Johansson made contact and, later, Villeneuve ran at a vulnerable pace and such as Andretti and Gordon stormed by. Villeneuve complained of understeer, which made overtaking problematical. "We were expecting the car to go loose as the race went on but it didn't. The most important thing is that we finished and got some more points." Tracy 32, Villeneuve, Bobby Rahal (Rahal-Hogan/Lola) and Scott Pruett (Patrick Racing/Lola) 30, Gugelmin 28, Andretti 24.

Round 4, Long Beach. He qualified eleventh and, when nicely in fifth, retired after 34 laps: transmission.

Pruett 46, Gugelmin 38, Unser 34, Tracy 32, Rahal and Villeneuve 30.

Round 5, Nazareth. He qualified third and spent much of the race grappling with Emerson Fittipaldi. Andretti fell back, losing grip, and Villeneuve inherited the lead. He pitted just short of half distance. "Our first set of tyres was really strong. We were getting great mileage. There was no reason to stop until we ran out of fuel or the tyres wore out." Fittipaldi, emerging from a pit stop, took him and the race seemed to lie between them but Cheever was on a long, sustained thrust. With 40 laps left he caught Villeneuve who, lapping Danny Sullivan [PacWest/Reynard], had to go wide. Cheever pounced. Cheever intended to get to the end making one stop less than either Fittipaldi or Villeneuve: that gave him the lead but he ran out of fuel with two laps left.

At that instant the race did lie between Fittipaldi and Villeneuve — Villeneuve swarming. "The last few laps were an incredible battle with Jacques," Fittipaldi said. "His tyres were a little fresher than mine and I really had to work hard to keep him behind me. I was with Jacques for most of the race. He did an incredible drive." Fittipaldi one hour 31 minutes 23.41, Villeneuve one hour 31 minutes 23.71.

It was 23 April. Fittipaldi said he intended to return to Brazil and became emotionally distraught. "May 1 is going to be the one year anniversary of the tragedy when we lost Ayrton Senna. I want to dedicate this victory to his memory."

Pruett 51, Villeneuve 47, Rahal and Gugelmin 38, Emerson Fittipaldi 35.

Car control, 1995 (Ray Giguere/Canapress).

Round 6, Indianapolis. Before the month began Villeneuve travelled to Milan to accept a motorsport award. *La Stampa* journalist Christiano Chiavegato says: "It's what we call a *Prime* and I'm on the jury. Every year we nominate one person. We had Michael Schumacher one time, Patrick Head [the Williams Technical Director] another. In 1995 it was Villeneuve. He gave a long interview, he spoke about himself, about his feeling for racing. He said 'I don't want to come to Formula 1 too early.' He was very, very quiet. He said 'I don't dream Ferrari, I don't dream of being like my father. I want to be myself, Jacques Villeneuve. If this season is good in IndyCars I may do another.'" Thence to the month on the rack.

Cicale is sure that "in his own mind I think Jacques expected to win Indy, not necessarily the second year but early on in his career, and he expected to be IndyCar champion and in many ways he expects to be Formula 1 champion; but I don't think he put or puts a time-frame on them."

The portents were not immediately good at Indianapolis. As practice got serious Luyendyk broke the track record with a lap of 234.107mph and his Menard team-mate Brayton went into the stratosphere too. On the Friday before Pole Day Villeneuve crashed in Turn Two while trying to pass a slower car on cold tyres. On the Saturday the weather was so bad Pole Day was extended into the Sunday. He qualified fifth.

Brayton	231.604mph
Luyendyk	231.031
Goodyear	230.759
Andretti	229.294
Villeneuve	228.397

Unser and Fittipaldi of the mighty Penskes didn't qualify at all and that hadn't happened to the team since they'd first entered in 1969.

Maybe that set the tone for the completely unexpected. You can never tell. At the start Andretti surged up behind Goodyear and Luyendyk but immediately the world went mad. From the fourth row Fox — an Indianapolis specialist in the sense that he rarely competed in other IndyCar events — went low into Turn One and may have run over the rumble strips there. At some 200mph the car veered

. . . the Canadians — Bourbonnais, Patrick Carpentier, Villeneuve, Empringham, Greg Moore (Frank Gunn/ Canapress).

Tapestry of Toronto: giving Sandrine a lift (Moe Doiron/ Canapress).

into and over Cheever and struck the wall an immense blow. Fox was taken to hospital with serious head injuries.

The re-start came after nine laps. Andretti led at **35**, pitted just before yellow for debris in Turn One. Goodyear pitted, too, passing the lead suddenly and unexpectedly to Villeneuve. That proved to be one of the most controversial and unexpected events in the recent history of the Indy 500. We'd better examine it in detail, misunderstandings, traumas and all.

"I didn't know I was in the lead at that point," Villeneuve said. "Everybody was flying by the pace car and I didn't see him wave to me." Nor, Villeneuve insisted, did he see a wave next time round but "the third time he was really waving so I hit the brakes. I didn't know he was talking to me because I didn't know I was in the lead."

Clarification. The yellows are flags — and also lights which, typically, are placed on the outside wall, of which, at Indianapolis, there are a dozen. Indianapolis PR director Bob Walters explains: "We are 100% computer wired here and, optically, video wired. We have a timing and scoring monitor which means you know exactly where you are at any given point. There's television available and I don't know whether they were watching TV or not in that pit but they had a thing that showed Jacques in 'P1' and they chose to not believe that. They were sure they had him a lap down and that all of our computer scoring was inaccurate.

"There's a guy that sits in the right-hand seat of the pace car and he's got bright yellow gloves on and rule one is, no matter what, you don't pass the pace car unless you are real sure that guy in the pace car is giving you a wave-by sign. Jacques' people will tell you that he got the wave-by sign. He did not. What he got was the racing slow-down sign with the palms faced towards the ground and you could see that pretty easily on television. His pit told him to pass the pace car, that he was a lap down" — the assumption being the pace car would naturally allow drivers by until it had picked up the leader, *then* make the field bunch. "There were a couple of cars that had been waved by because they were behind Jacques. You never pass the pace car unless he tells you to. It's like you don't pass a police car — well, in the States you don't."

Right . . . *Villeneuve power* (Pierre Labrie/Canapress).

142

The pits are closed under yellows until the bunching behind the pace car is complete. Villeneuve — circling — could not come in until 42, almost out of fuel. Three laps later he was given a two-lap penalty for passing the pace car. Chief Steward Tom Binford said: "It was a flagrant violation. I think there were three instances when the pace car tried to wave him down. He just didn't slow down."

What happened from Team Green's point of view? "We were running in third place a lap before the yellow," Cicale says. "Jacques was aware of his position because we not only gave it to him on the radio but we also gave it to him on the pit board. Unfortunately a lot of times he didn't like to look at the pit board. He relied on the radio transmission.

"Basically, before the yellow in question we were not in the lead. A lap before the yellow, unbeknown to us, Scott Goodyear came in to the pits [and Andretti, too] for fuel. Then there was this yellow and you're not allowed to come in until everybody packs up [bunches] behind the pace car. We were scheduled to come in on the lap that the yellow was shown. We only had a gallon, a gallon and a half of fuel left in the car. Probably what Jacques saw on the pit board was 'P3.' In the confusion we may not have said — because we didn't realise — that Goodyear [and Andretti] had come in. As soon as we saw the yellow we said 'yellow, yellow, pack up behind the pace car. As soon as you're allowed to, come into the pits, come into the pits.'

"The pace car, in my estimation, didn't determine that Jacques was the leader, because he was not the leader before the yellow. I can remember — this may be a figment of my imagination — but I distinctly remember the pace car going by us, we were watching Jacques, I was talking to him on the radio. I said 'Jacques, we have to save fuel, run it in sixth gear, run the minimum revs you can.' We wanted to come in. We were running out of fuel. And of course if there's a yellow and the pace car stays out there for 10 laps and they don't open the pits, you could actually run out of fuel.

"I kept on saying 'Jacques, we have very little fuel, pack up behind the pace car as soon as you can, save as much fuel as you can.' I was adamant about that because that was our critical condition at the time. What I recall is the pace car going by us in the pits and waving Jacques by as well as everybody else. So Jacques said 'the pace car waved me by.' We didn't think twice about it because we didn't think he was leading.

"What happens is the pace car waves everybody through until they find the leader, then they supposedly hold out their hand and don't wave it any more but hold it rigidly out and stop the leader. I don't think they knew Jacques was the leader until after they had already waved him by. He went by the pace car twice, as did everybody else, and finally they determined he was in fact the leader. They held out the hand, stopped him, he was then the leader of the race. Everybody packed up behind him, they opened the pits, and we had no fuel at all. I mean absolutely none. He'd done five or six laps under the yellow and fortunately you have the ability to lean the engine down considerably and you get quite good fuel mileage — but no fuel in the car whatsoever. It ran out coming down the pit lane . . .

I'd discuss different possibilities, so we both knew what might happen and what to do

---

"Jacques went back out still under the yellow and the USAC officials [United States Auto Club, running the event] came up to us and said 'we are penalising Jacques two laps because he passed the pace car.' We said '*what???* No way. They waved him by.' And we fought and fought and fought and of course you can't do anything with USAC. They make the decision and that's it, end of story. From that point on we said to Jacques 'look, we're two laps down.' We were all obviously discouraged because we'd been running so well. We said 'look, we're going to get one lap back at a time. We'll just keep running as quickly as we can, we'll stretch our fuel, we'll stretch our tyres as long as we can. We won't stop under this half-tank scenario that most teams do, we'll stay out' — and of course when you stay out you normally pick up extra laps [as others pit].

"He came into the pits two times after that totally, absolutely out of fuel and totally, absolutely out of tyres because we also went with a softer Goodyear tyre. That increased our speed a great deal through the race and allowed us to get our two laps back." Villeneuve confesses to "swearing a little bit" when he heard the penalty and concentrated his thinking on getting to the finish, searching out a point or two towards the championship; no other way to think when two laps equal five miles — in Formula 1 the equivalent of more than a complete lap of the longest circuit, Spa. Green was reported at the time as radioing *we're not out of this, let's stay concentrated*. During my interview Green said "that's right. We rallied even the guys in the pits. I mean, everyone's down. We went from the lowest of lows to the highest of highs and that was purely because we rallied everyone. And it wasn't just me. Obviously I do most of the talking on the radio. Jacques didn't talk to us as much as we talked to him. He wanted the information coming to him, he didn't tell us quite as much. He knew what he was doing. Anyway, 25 laps later, 30 laps later, whatever it was, we've got one of our laps back. He was determined."

Cicale gives the overall context. "If a yellow comes out, 75 or 80% of the time you'll just say to the driver 'come in.' Your decisions in IndyCar have to be instantaneous because, for example, a lap at Phoenix is 19 seconds so if you're half way around the track you have only nine and a half seconds before the driver is in the pits if you want him in. The decisions have to be almost pre-thought out. In fact a lot of my race engineering was spent on Sunday mornings going over the race lap by lap before it happened and saying 'what would happen if there was a yellow here, what would happen if we had a punctured tyre there?' I really had to go through that in my own mind to try to come up with the permutations so I would react to a situation. Your decision has to be virtually gut feeling. It's not really very scientific. I'd discuss the different possibilities with Jacques so that we both had a clear understanding of what might happen in the race and what we would do if it did happen."

The advantage of this preparation wasn't long in coming. Under yellow on **80** Villeneuve and Gugelmin, the leader, pitted. Villeneuve emerged quicker than Gugelmin, thereby reducing the deficit to one lap. What follows may seem a bewildering profusion (and probably is) but it's also the essence of IndyCar racing.

On **117** Gugelmin pitted again but Villeneuve didn't and at **123** a car halted on the circuit. Under this yellow Villeneuve did pit, got

Right . . . *third, but you still get to spray the champagne* (Robert Laberge/Canapress).

146

out in 'front' of Gugelmin and thus unlapped himself. He ran tenth, 14 seconds behind Gugelmin.

A clutch of cars pitted at the next yellow — **138** — so that Jimmy Vasser (Ganassi/Reynard) led, Villeneuve second. When they were released from the yellow on **141** he lay three and a half seconds from Vasser, with Goodyear and Pruett some distance behind him. Vasser extended his lead to seven seconds by **153**. Vasser pitted — and Villeneuve led, holding that to **163** when he moved towards the pits himself under yellow; but the pitlane had already closed and he had to scrabble to regain the track. In that time Pruett and Goodyear had gone by. He was third.

Villeneuve pitted two laps later, virtually no fuel in the tank; Pruett and Goodyear came in too, returning the lead to Vasser. Pruett attacked but, overtaking in Turn Three, forced Vasser off line. Vasser clipped the wall, bringing out the yellow. As the pace car released them Goodyear hammered past Pruett and led for nine laps, victory in sight, Villeneuve third. On **185** Pruett skimmed over oil, spun and glanced the wall. They circled behind the pace car for four laps, leaving a lunge to the flag.

The pace car was in Turn Four and preparing to peel off as Goodyear was in Turn Three. It's a ritual thing, a fast-on-the-draw equation to maximise the moment when the pace car does peel off: a balancing of anticipation and not putting the hammer down a fraction too soon. Goodyear pressed the accelerator hard but reached the pace car before it was anywhere near the pit lane entry and passed it.

Clarification. "You don't pass the pace car," Walters says. "The entire world saw Goodyear pass the pace car. He was trying to part the field. Once the pace car turns its lights off, which would be on the back straightaway, it pulls away from the field to get out of the way. The pack is then under the control of whoever's in front of it. Goodyear was leading it, he was crawling along about 50mph, and that's normal. What you're trying to do is take off and the guy behind can't catch you: he doesn't get a jump on you. That's what Scott was doing. He let the pace car get all the way to Turn Four, he lit his tyres, left a 75 yard burn-out stripe behind both tyres — you could see it, black lines coming out of the back of the car — and all of a sudden

Right *Just plain serious* (Robert Laberge/Canapress).

he's going 120. Through Turn Four he averaged 202mph and the track was still yellow. He went flying by the pace car. He mis-timed his take off." There was criticism that the pace car was travelling too slowly — normally, as Kirby says, the objective is "to get the hell out of it" — but equally that Goodyear had been too aggressive.

Villeneuve saw Goodyear "overtake the pace car and I knew he was in trouble. That's why I jumped on the brakes [and almost caused a multiple crash]. A regulation is a regulation. The green came on as we came out of Turn Four, but Scott passed the pace car in the Turn."

Goodyear mounted a stout defence. "When you were following the pace car, if you slowed to let him pull away he'd slow to let you catch up. The slower I'd go the slower he'd go and I'd find myself coming back to him. I let him go until I couldn't see him and then when I went by I saw him on the apron [infield]. The next light I saw was green."

Goodyear was black-flagged from **193** (a black flag anywhere in the world orders a driver to the pits immediately, no argument). Goodyear ignored it because he reasoned he had nothing to lose by staying out and much to gain. He was wrong. He completed the race but officials had stopped counting his laps from **195**, making him fourteenth.

Villeneuve, second on the road — as the saying goes — had won.

"As the race went on we made some changes to the car which made it better. We came back and we got the yellows at the right time, although I did screw up twice in the pits. First I started to go before they finished fuelling and then next time I stalled it. We did everything we could *not* to win this race . . ."

How did Jacques take the win?

"He was fine," Cicale says. "In many ways Jacques doesn't show much emotion. After the race he was happy enough, he was joyous but he wasn't overwhelmed. I mean, Indianapolis is one of those races where you're there for three weeks. We run a huge amount of the time and there's a tremendous amount of pressure to perform there on a regular basis. Consequently, in all honesty, once the race comes all you really want is to get it over with. All you want is to finish the bloody thing and go home. That was my feeling at the end of winning the Indy 500. *It's finally over.* I really had not much more feeling then than if we had finished second or third or fifth or ninth.

You always go away from that race saying to yourself *it's finally finished, the stupid thing.*"

A poignant and almost inevitable post-script. Vince Laughran of the Russell School says that "a US television commentator asked Jacques about his thoughts of his father in the closing laps of the race. I am paraphrasing but, in effect, the commentator wanted to know about that" — meaning was he thinking of his father? "Jacques replied 'absolutely not. I was thinking about the team, I was thinking about the car holding together.'

Villeneuve 67, Rahal 52, Pruett 51, Gugelmin 47, Gordon 43.

Round 7, Milwaukee. Anti-climax. He qualified eleventh and moved solidly to sixth, three laps down on the winner, Tracy.

Villeneuve 75, Gordon 53, Pruett, Rahal and Tracy 52, Unser 51.

Round 8, Detroit. A curious race. He qualified ninth and finished ninth, though not before Tracy had "wheel-banged" past, the gearshift had played up and he'd made an extra pit stop. The first time into the pits Villeneuve had been forced to stop wide of the pit

Victory at Cleveland, 1995 (Robert Laberge/Canapress).

markings because of an airhose left in the wrong place.

Villeneuve 79, Gordon 75, Pruett 66, Unser 61, Tracy 57.

Round 9, Portland. Phillips reported: "Unser harried pole-winner Villeneuve into a mistake at quarter-distance, then pulled away to a commanding lead from Villeneuve and Paul Tracy. Tracy subsequently got around Villeneuve in traffic on lap 51, before the Indy 500 winner fell out of second place with a broken shock absorber mount." Villeneuve and Gordon 81, Andretti 69, Rahal 68, Pruett 67, Unser 61.

Round 10, Elkhart Lake. He asserted himself and began to mould a championship. He took pole and Cicale prepared a plan: setting the car up with low downforce to exploit the car's top speed. Cicale pointed out that, with three 200mph straights, cornering was not critical. "Face it, when it comes to racing what matters is how fast you go on the straights and how well you brake. That's how you pass and stay ahead of people."

Villeneuve led throughout. "The gearbox was OK although the rear end was a little light early on. If we'd been racing wheel-to-wheel I might have had some problems but I never had to push too hard. We were able to get a good lead and when you can do that you can conserve tyres, brakes and fuel." Because the Green team was comparatively small, Villeneuve explained that "the whole group just has to work harder. It's one thing to have a fast car but it has to feel right to the driver. It's very important to work well with the team, more important than to have an advantage with an engine or chassis." Villeneuve 103, Gordon 81, Rahal 78, Tracy and Pruett 73.

Round 11, Toronto. In qualifying Villeneuve was quickest both days and said the car felt strong, the favourite word. No driver had taken three successive pole positions since 1992 (Rahal). He finished third. "We had a little bad luck when the first yellow came out too late, but Michael [Andretti, winner] and Bobby [Rahal, second] were faster anyway." Villeneuve 118, Rahal 94, Gordon 91, Andretti 90, Tracy 78.

Round 12, Cleveland. Front row and then uproar. De Ferran led most of the race. "We didn't have enough downforce and after a few laps my car began sliding around," Villeneuve said. He slipped to sixth. "In the middle of the race, on full tanks, we had a lot of understeer in the long right-hander onto the front straight and oversteer in the corner before that. Sometimes you have to hang on in there. When you're leading the points you can't do anything stupid."

From a great deal of crashing and bashing (by other people) Andretti led with three laps to go but slowed with an engine problem. Bryan Herta (Ganassi/Reynard) seized the lead but under yellow. Herta *thought* he'd overtaken Andretti under the yellow — which had come out for a crash. He couldn't see the yellow any more but he *could* see the crashed car still there. Herta "slowed and put my hand up to let Michael by." Herta understood that if you made such a mistake under a yellow, and did allow the other guy back past, it counted as an atonement.

Between IndyCar rounds, Jacques flew to England to test the Williams

---

While this was going on Villeneuve struck and helped himself to the lead but Andretti banged wheels with him trying to get it back. Andretti faded and Herta finished second. Gordon, who'd been in the midst of the earlier barging, received an admonition from Villeneuve: "It's great that the racing is so competitive but it doesn't have to be dirty." Villeneuve 138, Rahal 106, Gordon 99, Andretti 96, Tracy 78.

Round 13, Michigan. He qualified fourth but spent 15 laps in the pits when a rear wheel bearing failed. He slogged to tenth.

Villeneuve 141, Rahal 111, Gordon 99, Andretti 96, Pruett 93.

Between this and the next round Villeneuve flew to England and tested the Williams at Silverstone. Williams were interested in Villeneuve and Villeneuve was interested in Williams.

Round 14, Mid Ohio. Pole again although he crashed twice in qualifying, the first time when the team were experimenting with new suspension parts, the second "when I got too greedy" trying to improve on his pole time — half a second quicker than Herta. And, as it seemed, the championship was tumbling into his lap without much more moulding needed. At one point he slid into Rahal but still finished third. Andretti's engine let go and Rahal was out, after hitting a wall.

Villeneuve 156, Rahal 111, Gordon 104, Andretti and Unser 97.

Between Mid Ohio and the next race Williams confirmed that Villeneuve had signed for them for 1996. It had been swiftly done. Williams liked Villeneuve and Villeneuve liked Williams.

Round 15, New Hampshire. It didn't go well in qualifying and during the race he drove to a steady fourth ("the car was strong and the only problem I had was after the first 15 laps, oversteer"), Andretti second, Rahal tenth but Unser was appealing his disqualification from Portland: he'd won but the Penske failed scrutineering with a technical infringement. The appeal was expected to be heard soon and, if successful, would give Unser 21 points and wrest one from Villeueuve. This did not disturb the ultimate simplicity. Unser needed a mathematical miracle to take the championship from Villeneuve: Rahal and Andretti were now out of it.

Villeneuve 168, Rahal 114, Andretti 113, Unser 111, Gordon 108.

Round 16, Vancouver. The Unser appeal was postponed to 18 September, which meant after the end of the season. In qualifying however, it seemed Villeneuve had rendered that meaningless by going fastest both days: pole worth one lovely point. Sixth place became good enough for the championship. He was fourth when the gearbox misbehaved, losing 5th and 6th gears. The car would do no more than 120mph on the straights and he finished twelfth, a couple of laps adrift of the winner . . . Unser.

Green said "we let Jacques down. We wanted to go to Laguna with a chance just to race. Now we have to go there and fight it out. We have to be sure. But my hat's off to Al Jnr and Team Penske — they did exactly what they needed to do." Villeneuve felt it was "a little ridiculous" that the Unser appeal was delayed. "I don't think it's very professional in a tough series like IndyCar."

Villeneuve 170, Unser 132, Rahal 124, Gordon 122, Andretti 113.

Round 17, Laguna Seca. Villeneuve pole, Unser fourteenth — potentially crippling but in the matrix of an IndyCar race, with all its in-built uncertainties and possibilities, who knew? Nobody.

"We approached every race the same," Cicale says. "We took it one race at a time. We really didn't look for anything other than doing the best that we could. We weren't really sure if Jnr was getting his

Right *Vancouver, with the championship beckoning, was a problem.*
Villeneuve prepares (Ray Giguere/Canapress).

points back or not. That went on and on and on. We said 'well, we want to be in front of Jnr' and he's a funny guy, old Jnr, he could qualify fourteenth and still win the race, like he's done many times. We never, ever count him out. So we went into that race saying 'we want to win the race.' It was funny. We really didn't feel a huge amount of pressure because deep down we never thought CART [Championship Auto Racing Teams, who run the championship] would reverse its decision and give Jnr his points back.

"We didn't have any illusions about anything except doing the best we could. Jacques approached it in that light as well, very calm. Another place, another race. That was it. That's one of his greatest strengths. He doesn't seem to be intimidated by situations, intimidated by people, intimidated by his environment. He just sits down and gets on with the job. It's incredible, really and one thing he's unique at. I know if it was me or any other ordinary individual, we would react totally differently: we'd be upset, we'd panic, we'd be worried about it. Maybe deep down he does feel it but certainly it's nothing that he shows externally."

Villeneuve outheaved Herta to the first corner and led, Unser galloping as he would have to do. His imperative: to win or take second. Unser rose but reached a "road block" of three cars contesting seventh place — Andre Ribeiro [Tasman/Reynard], Andretti and Rahal — and made a strategic pit stop; galloped on and was ninth when Rahal pitted.

Villeneuve came in on lap 35 (of the 84) — a punctured left front tyre — dropping him to eleventh. "It wasn't a great feeling but we knew we were still in the race." Unser was now fifth and within sight of Gugelmin, fourth; and became fourth while Villeneuve — tenth — came in again on lap 45, a punctured left front again. "When we blew the second one we were still OK," Villeneuve said.

Green thought "some debris was getting between the brake duct and the sidewall, cutting the tyre. Either that or, because we had quite a bit of understeer and you tend to turn in early with that, it's easy to hook the tyre on the inside edge of the track." Unser third.

Villeneuve said that "exactly the same thing happened both times. The car started pulling to one side and the steering started getting heavy. I really noticed it at the turn going up the hill on the back part of the track. I had to struggle to turn the car because it was bottoming-out." Worse, five laps later, Villeneuve ran over debris and came in *again*. That really "took us out" because it was "a longer pit stop." He went a lap down and fell as low as fourteenth, rose to finish eleventh. It was, as it proved, enough.

Unser, held by the logic of his situation, "hustled" too much to make up time and destroyed his tyres before his second stop. The logic of that was also simple. He lost time before the stop and never regained it. Sixth place at the end was scant consolation.

Villeneuve was the youngest IndyCar Champion since 1952.

"It was a fun race," Villeneuve said, almost laconically. "We had to drive aggressively and pass some cars, so it *was* fun." He paid sincere tribute to Green and the team and used the word fun a third time. Unser's Portland win would be reinstated, but that evening it was Villeneuve 173, Unser 140, Rahal 130, Andretti 125, Gordon 122.

Pete Spence of Cosinc — the American arm of Cosworth engine manufacturing — reflects on his three years with Villeneuve. "He appears to be a much more balanced individual than his father,

Staying close to the wall (Ray Giguere/Canapress).

although I didn't know his father at all [except by reputation, as every motorsport follower does]. Gilles seemed to be living on the ragged edge. Jacques obviously loves the speed and so on but he says 'you know, I am not going to do this for ever. I am not crazy. I like it right now but I don't see it as the be-all and end-all of life.'

"Sometimes it is obvious he is young but we have all watched him mature greatly over the past couple of years. I think it would be advantageous for him to have a mentor, like Patrick Head, for example, to represent a father figure. The situation as I saw it was that Tony Cicale was really his father for the last two years [Cicale intended to quit racing but stayed because of Villeneuve]. Although Jacques has been brought up in this racing environment . . . well, I watched the pressure and the stress that was on Ayrton. At the end of every session he couldn't get from the garage to the motorhome without there being a mass of fans and TV cameras poking into his face. If there is a time when that becomes too much, you need someone to talk to.

"That said, Jacques has a very good personality, a very good approach to the whole thing, he's been brought up with it so he is not overawed by it. It is not a foreign environment to him and he is much less likely to be fazed by it. Typically, he is consistent, light on fuel, easy on the car, quick-witted, very aware of tyre conditions — and these are qualities that you have to have. You also have to have that self-belief and that is what Ayrton had. Ayrton's philosophy was *there is no reason why I shouldn't get through this corner at 180 miles an hour* — an ultimate self-belief. If you have any self-doubt you won't commit to the corner at the speed you need. I believe Jacques has the same. There is enough arrogance there, if you like. Look at Michael Schumacher. It often manifests itself as arrogance to get to the necessary edge."

Fun?

"I remember Jacques getting bollockings from Barry Green for not being ready to get in the car just before races. He'd be standing on the grid and he had to go for a pee like three minutes before the start, which is ridiculous! We had a bathroom in our support truck. Jacques would set off running and I'd point him in the direction of the truck . . ."

CHAPTER FIVE

Trans-Atlantic

IT BRINGS US back to the August day at Silverstone in 1995 which could only make the comparison between father and son sharper than it had ever been before. In the most poignant sense they were meeting on equal ground: Formula 1. It was a Tuesday.

Jacques Villeneuve had driven in the Michigan 500 on the Sunday and caught the overnight London flight from Chicago. He went to the Williams factory with his manager, Craig Pollock, to sort out the precise details of the test and have a seat fitting. Then he went to an hotel in Buckingham, nicely handy for Silverstone, and slept soundly.

Silverstone was not as his father would have remembered it although the general contours remained unaltered. The track still unfolded in the same direction but virtually all the corners had been truncated. The circuit of immense, unadulterated speed — the push-pump-push through Stowe, the gathering thunder through Club, the scream through Abbey — lay among memories. Silverstone was a geometrical and technical examination now.

Villeneuve approached this, and the comparison, evenly. He also approached evenly the more direct comparison with resident Williams driver Damon Hill. At 11.05 on this Tuesday he accelerated out of the pit lane and completed two laps, feeling his way. Then he got down to it: 20 more laps in the morning, 35 in the afternoon.

Giving feed-back at the Silverstone testing (ICN U.K. Bureau).

With the seat slightly wrong — he was moving fractionally around, but that's important — and using an old specification Renault engine he got to within a second of Hill's best time. He'd enjoyed himself, he said, but the gearchange on the steering wheel was unfamiliar and "a bit like a computer game."

It was a general testing day. Here are some comparisons.

	Morning	Afternoon
Hill	1:30.94	1:29.14
Villeneuve	1:34.46	1:30.02
Eddie Irvine (Jordan)	1:31.37	1:31.59
Mika Hakkinen (McLaren)	1:32.74	1:31.82
Martin Brundle (Ligier)	1:33.22	1:34.03

Reflecting, Villeneuve would say: "The Formula 1 car is much lighter than the IndyCar and you can play a little more with it although it is not as stable. It is much quicker in the corners and the braking is much better. The overall acceleration down the straight is similar, maybe a little bit less, although that is difficult to judge: at some tracks you use very long gears. Because it does not have a turbo, the power is there right away."

The Williams personnel were impressed by the feedback Villeneuve was able to give, impressed by how "easy going" he was, and Villeneuve himself added "we had a few laughs as well."

On the Wednesday, the seat now better, Villeneuve did one minute 31.74 against Hill's one minute 30.04. On the Thursday Hill was replaced by the other resident Williams driver, David Coulthard. In the morning Villeneuve proved quicker but towards the end of the afternoon Coulthard cranked up the pace. With a few minutes of the day remaining Villeneuve prepared to have a tilt but forgot to switch the fuel pump on and the climax became anti-climax.

	Morning	Afternoon
Coulthard	1:30.80	1:28.69
Villeneuve	1:30.78	1:29.72
Irvine	1:31.52	1:31.33
Ukyo Katayama (Tyrrell)	1:32.39	No time
Hakkinen	1:32.69	1:32.01

Villeneuve's times would compare well with the Williams drivers David Coulthard and Damon Hill (ICN U.K. Bureau).

There's always a temptation to regard testing as a sort of race, with the times giving the result. Times do have a validity, but only in the context of what a team or a driver is trying to do. Villeneuve demonstrated, to himself as well as the team, that he could handle the car (only one spin, remember) and exploit it. Whatever the true context of Silverstone might have been, he was on the pace. The 1:29.72 would have translated to the third row of the grid for the British Grand Prix a month before, quicker than Johnny Herbert in the Benetton and Jean Alesi in the Ferrari. Nor must we forget that Villeneuve and the team were happy to have a tilt at Coulthard's 1:28.69, just to see.

Cumulatively the test stirred a sharp question. Would Villeneuve join Williams for 1996? He said he anticipated a decision soon but "I don't care when I announce it. That will depend on me." These words hold implications. He wasn't desperate to get into Formula 1 and he was his own man. Cumulatively, that's impressive, too. Why Williams? "They asked me, there were talks with other teams but I think this was the most serious one."

After the death of Senna, Williams had brought in Coulthard (who at the end of 1995 was leaving for McLaren). If Senna had not been killed, there would have been no immediate vacancy for Coulthard and, in direct succession to Coulthard, presumably no vacancy for Villeneuve either. It was a time of much change: Schumacher moving from Benetton to Ferrari, Gerhard Berger and Jean Alesi from Ferrari to Benetton.

The announcement came a week after Silverstone: Villeneuve was joining Williams for 1996. He rationalised his reasoning. "I wanted to go with a top team and now I have the opportunity. If I had decided to stay in IndyCars it would have closed doors to me in Formula 1 down the road, so we decided now was the time to do it. I'm sure I'll miss IndyCars and Team Green quite a lot."

Cicale had no doubts it was the right move, although before we reach that he recounts an amusing anecdote. "Jacques rang me and we chatted and he talked about the difference in braking in Formula 1, which is much, much greater than in IndyCars. I first realised that when I went to a Canadian Grand Prix at Montreal and I thought

Right *Villeneuve testing at Monza* (ICN U.K. Bureau).

these cars are never going to stop! He said he braked a little later each time and he could feel what he was doing."

Cicale knows "there were some sceptics who said it was a little early for Jacques to go into Formula 1 but I felt that it wasn't. I encouraged Jacques, really, to go. I said 'if you want to go that route you have a good opportunity to do it. Do it. Don't wait another year.' I encouraged him because I thought that ultimately he wanted to do that so I felt the sooner the better. He is not intimidated by anybody. He feels very, very European. Maybe one of Michael Andretti's problems [Andretti came from IndyCars to McLaren in 1993 and failed] was that he should have moved to England, lived and breathed it, made a total commitment to it. And of course Michael had bad luck at the start [with crashes and mechanical failures] when a little bit of good luck might have made all the difference."

Canadians believe he is better than his father, with greater long-range potential

In the midst of all this, I sought out a long-time Formula 1 follower and sometime journalist Peter Dick of Toronto to give me the Canadian context of Villeneuve, something I couldn't possibly deduce for myself, particularly since he seemed arguably more European than Canadian. [Revealingly, perhaps, Dick did not mention the fact that Villeneuve is French Canadian — and, shortly before, Quebec had voted to stay within Canada by a paltry 50,000 votes, so it might have been something to mention. I strongly suspect, and have always suspected, that while motor racing has nationalistic dimensions it is completely indifferent to politics.] This is what Dick said:

"I remember how I felt about Gilles. I had been following Formula 1 for almost a decade and never even considered that a Canadian would ever make it to there, nor distinguish themselves in it. There was no-one on the horizon and no apparent infrastructure to develop talent and prepare it for the international stage. I was used to seeing someone like George Eaton [a wealthy Canadian] buy himself a ride in the Canadian Grand Prix in the early 1970s, and that was about it. When Gilles went to Ferrari all of Canada seemed to hop on for the ride. It was the first, and only, time I remember distinct feelings of nationalistic pride. When I read European publications like *Autosport* or *Autocourse* repeatedly mentioning the 'brilliant Canadian' I felt proud. Some indication of the stature he attained can be illustrated by the fact that his funeral was televised live to the country and the then-Prime Minister, Pierre Trudeau, walked at his funeral.

"I have not felt that since, not even with guys like Paul Tracy winning in IndyCar racing. It was nice to see a Canadian winning presence, and between Jacques, Paul and Scott Goodyear there has been a Canadian 'invasion' in Indy racing over the last few years but I guess I never saw Paul, or Scott for that matter, as *the one*.

"Villeneuve wasn't really in the public consciousness too much until he and Team Green moved into IndyCar racing for their rookie year of 1994. I'd been aware of his name in some Italian Formula 3 races and I knew he was doing Formula Atlantic in 1993, winning a few races, but at that point I don't believe he had distinguished himself as anything special. It was '94 that did it. I remember him qualifying on the front row at Phoenix, and then the way he finished second in the Indianapolis 500 — reaping praise from all for his measured, disciplined and intelligent drive — really did bring him to our attention. The day he won his first race that year, at Elkhart Lake (the most demanding of road courses) after aggressively passing the likes of Al Unser Jnr and Paul Tracy, was when I knew he was *the one*.

"I believe that Canadians believe he is better than his father and has much greater long-range potential. The passage of time has given most people a slightly more balanced view of Gilles. Everyone speaks of his incredible brilliance, his raw gift in the car, but everyone also speaks of how he was a 'wild man,' showing very little in the way of 'intelligence' in the car. This made him, in hindsight, not a 'complete' driver. The perception is that Jacques has his father's gift but is a disciplined thinker.

"I don't like to be nationalistic too much. I see club mentality as destructive, divisive and I think it fosters the brickhead mentality kind of hooliganism we've seen from British fans at Silverstone in Mansell's day, or at some European soccer matches. Having said that, I get involuntary pangs of pride when I hear international studies claim Canada to be the best country in the world to live in and I am similarly getting those pangs every time Jacques amazes us and does us proud. The feeling here is that despite the year just passed [1995], this is only the very beginning. The nation is wishing him a collective *bonne chance*."

Villeneuve took the IndyCar Championship at Laguna Seca on 10 September. He returned to Europe to test at Monza, covering 38 laps on the Wednesday afternoon. "Once we got going it went pretty well. The only thing I have to do here is get the mileage and get used to the track and the car. There is not much work to do on the car itself." His best time was one minute 27.11 (worth the sixth row at the Italian Grand Prix). On the Thursday, covering 88 laps, he improved from 1:25.6 to 1:25.04 (worth the second row). Then he gave his overall thoughts.

Was it a big decision to come to Formula 1?

"It was a big decision. It is not only changing team, it is changing series and continents. I have been with Team Green in North America for three years and there was a great working relationship going on. I knew we would get good results the year after and so on, but the chance that I got to come into Formula 1 with Williams Renault is an opportunity that you can't just put aside. It is something that is very good if everything is the way you want. I always said I would not come to Formula 1 at any cost, so it had to be with a team that was out to win races and maybe championships, and for sure Williams is the best team!"

Did winning the IndyCar Championship make the decision easier?

"No, the results didn't change anything. For sure, leaving a series it is better to leave with a championship and some important wins, but it didn't come into the decision. What changed it though — well, the win in Indy [the 500] for example opened the eyes of the European people quite a lot more, so it did have an effect, but not on my personal decision."

Are you looking forward to the challenge of Formula 1?

"Oh yes, definitely. There is a lot to learn and it is going to be very different. All the tracks and the cars are very different and it is going to be a whole new bunch of drivers that for the most part I haven't raced against. I have raced against a few in F3 but you can't really compare it. It's a big challenge but, with the fact that the IndyCar

Right *Mastering Monza, September 1995* (ICN U.K. Bureau).

season finished a week ago, I have plenty of time to get a lot of mileage done before next season. I hope to be ready. I don't want to get into the season just sitting back and not fighting with the quickest. That is not how I want to get into Formula 1."

A thought I put to Barry Green: *In three years you took him from being a kid to IndyCar Champion.*

"I don't say and I can't say Barry Green did that. I have got to say the team did that. Everyone had a lot of input. The only good thing I did right was hire all the good people that were scattered around Jacques, like Tony Cicale, and the crew and my brother, who is team manager. We all had input. Now Jacques and I and Craig were, I think, very close."

The leaving?

"Well, obviously I was shattered, but no-one had promised me something and not lived up to the promise. We had a three-year deal, we never ever had a four-year deal. We were in the middle of negotiating a fourth year. I hadn't agreed upon anything and he hadn't agreed upon anything except we'd agreed on terms *if* we decided to do it. I'd gone back to all the sponsors and gotten the increases that I needed and gotten everything approved, so we had everything in place from our side. I have to believe he was somewhat torn over what to do.

"He was having fun over here but at the same time he looked like winning the championship, he just won the Indy 500. He had no choice, the way I saw it. Once they made him the offer where the numbers were agreeable to him . . . well, what would have happened if he'd stayed and had a bad year? Those offers might disappear for three or four years. But once he'd decided I was very upset. I still go on record today [January 1996] saying I'm not sure he's ready to run a Grand Prix race.

"I said we would definitely lose him to Formula 1, because I believe he's that good, but I am not the person to say he's ready to go to Formula 1 yet. He's a brilliant young driver and he will be brilliant in Formula 1 some time but I don't know when that will be. Maybe it will be '96. But I'm not the guy who has to stand up there and say it so I'm reserving my judgement. He said he wanted his approach to

Right *Waiting for rain* (ICN U.K. Bureau).

Formula 1 to be the same as it had been to IndyCar. He was well prepared before the first IndyCar race.

"But getting back to the point, I was very disappointed and so were the team but I don't see how Jacques had a choice and I think he made the right choice. I'd gone out and raised all this extra money to cover what he needed and was very pleased with myself and then all of a sudden someone pulls the rug out from underneath me but I can't blame him. He did the right thing, he's a great friend of ours and we will certainly all be pulling for him at Williams. Our challenge then was just to survive."

We all know that motor racing is about arriving and leaving, not simply in the races but in general.

"Yes, yes, you deal with what you have got at the time and worry about tomorrow tomorrow."

You ran him from the age of 21 to 24. Did you feel he was growing up as a man?

"Oh, I think he grew up tremendously. I think when he arrived he had a big problem accepting the responsibility from the fans, the responsibility of looking after the fans of The Name. He learnt to live with that and is actually a natural now when he talks.

"It's very, very hard for the average fan to understand what Jacques puts into his job.

"He doesn't just drive the car. Jacques sits on computers for hours going through the data and suddenly remembering the third lap after he'd put new tyres on in qualifying, that he changed his line through Turn Four. He goes back to the computer and he figures out the answers to 'OK, was it better or worse? Where did it help?' He spent h-o-u-r-s on those computers. Many nights he would miss dinner because he was in on those computers. The fans don't realise that and it really hurt Jacques that he couldn't get that message across and didn't give the fans enough time. I saw him deal with that over the three years in a much, much better way and when he drives like he does on the racetrack he doesn't have to be . . ."

At this point, Green's voice trails away in admiration so I'll complete the sentence.

. . . doesn't have to be anything but the driver he is.

At Imola in early October Villeneuve ran for three days, taking over Hill's car on the last day and recording one minute 27.91. That was within a fraction of Hill's best, one minute 27.56 (and worth third row of the grid at the San Marino Grand Prix). Round Magny-Cours in mid-October he did 77 laps in a day with a best of one minute 17.61 (second row of the grid at the French Grand Prix).

At Estoril he ran for three days but perhaps the second was most significant.

	Morning	Afternoon
Villeneuve	1:20.94	1:20.96
Schumacher (Ferrari)	1:21.30	1:21.51
Berger (Benetton)	1:23.51	1:22.26

Schumacher, twice World Champion with Benetton and now exploring the Ferrari of his new team, represented a yardstick, no matter how many reservations you have to have about times in testing. Certainly the 1:20.96 would have been worth the second row of the grid at the Portuguese Grand Prix. There's another dimension and it brings us full circle. Williams might well have headed for home after Day Three but they lingered in the hope of rain. The team described the following day in a cryptic paragraph: "62 laps in very wet conditions for experience and tyre testing."

I've described Villeneuve's extensive test programme in some detail because the testing captured his past as well as opening up his future; not simply how he got here but why he could do what he could do when he did get here. Estoril seems a distillation of this.

Jacques Villeneuve, approaching Formula 1 systematically and rationally, was happy to wait a day if it might give him the experience in the wet, and he made the most of it. Gilles Villeneuve was scarcely like this. You gave him a car and he drove it to the absolute maximum, almost by reflex as it were, a tremendous blossoming of florid, natural, instinctive capability.

It's touching that something this mundane — hanging on in the hope of rain — should define the difference between the approach of the son and the father. From the beginning of Jacques Villeneuve's career virtually everything had defined the difference but it's a paradox that the mundane — a drab, empty day among the hillocks of Estoril — should do so with such clarity.

It did.

Jacques Villeneuve's career highlights

Key: DNQ = did not qualify; DNS = did not start;
DNF = did not finish; P = pole.

1988 Italian Touring Championship (Alfa Romeo 33)

25 Sept	Pergusa	10
9 Oct	Monza	DNF
23 Oct	Imola	14

1989 Italian Formula 3
except Monaco (Reynard-Alfa Romeo)

2 Apr	Vallelunga	DNQ
16 Apr	Magione	DNQ
6 May	Monaco F3	DNQ
15 May	Varano	DNQ
28 May	Pergusa	10
25 June	Monza	DNF
8 July	Vallelunga	DNQ
27 Aug	Misano	19
3 Sept	Monza	DNF
17 Sept	Imola	16
8 Oct	Vallelunga	DNF

1990 Italian Formula 3 (Reynard-Alfa Romeo)

1 Apr	Vallelunga	DNF
15 Apr	Pergusa	6
29 Apr	Magione	8
12 May	Varano	DNF
17 June	Imola	FL/5
24 June	Monza	DNF
8 July	Binetto	2
28 July	Misano	DNF
2 Sept	Monza	18
16 Sept	Varano	10
6 Oct	Vallelunga	10
21 Oct	Mugello	14

Championship: Roberto Colciago 38, Alessandro Zanardi 35, Massimiliano Angelelli 30 (Villeneuve 10, fourteenth).

1991 Italian Formula 3
except Monaco and Macau (Reynard-Alfa Romeo/
Ralt-Alfa Romeo from 5 May)

31 Mar	Misano	DNF
14 Apr	Binetto	DNF
21 Apr	Pergusa	8
5 May	Vallelunga	23
11 May	Monaco F3	DNF
19 May	Magione	4
1 June	Imola	P/4
15 June	Varano	DNQ
30 June	Monza	P/2
14 July	Mugello	24
1 Sept	Monza	P/3
15 Sept	Mugello	25
6 Oct	Vallelunga	3
24 Nov	Macau GP (F3)	8
1 Dec	Fuji*	8

*Championship: G Busi 44, D Schiattarella 38, A Gilardi 36 (Villeneuve 20, sixth). * Euro-Macau-Japan Challenge Cup F3*

1992 Japanese Formula 3 (Toyota)
except Group C at Mine (Toyota), Monaco F3 (Dallara-Alfa Romeo),
Macau F3 (Toyota), Formula Atlantic (Ralt-Toyota)

8 Mar	Suzuka	6
29 Mar	Tsukuba	4
3 May	Fuji	3
24 May	Suzuka	3
30 May	Monaco F3	9
14 June	Nishi-Sendai	1
28 June	Ti Circuit	3
12 July	Mine	1
14 Aug	Trois Rivieres F Atlantic	3
13 Sept	Sugo	4
27 Sept	Suzuka	P/2
25 Oct	Suzuka (non-Champ)	DNF
1 Nov	Mine Group C	2
15 Nov	Suzuka	P/1
22 Nov	Macau F3	3
29 Nov	Fuji F3	DNS

Championship: A Reid 55, Villeneuve 48, R Rydell 27.

1993 Formula Atlantic (Ralt-Toyota)
except Macau F3 (Ralt-Toyota)

4 Apr	Phoenix	DNF
18 Apr	Long Beach	P/2
9 May	Road Atlanta	P/1
6 June	Milwaukee	DNF
12 June	Montreal	1
20 June	Mosport	2
11 July	Halifax	DNF
18 July	Toronto	3
8 Aug	New Hampshire	P/2
15 Aug	Trois Rivieres	DNF
28 Aug	Vancouver	DNF
11 Sept	Mid Ohio	P/1
18 Sept	Nazareth	DNF
2 Oct	Laguna Seca	P/1

3 Oct	Laguna Seca	P/1
21 Nov	Macau F3	DNF

Championship: D Empringham 195, C Bourbonnais 191, Villeneuve 186.

1994 IndyCar Championship (Reynard-Cosworth)

20 Mar	Surfers' Paradise	17
10 Apr	Phoenix	DNF
17 Apr	Long Beach	15
29 May	Indianapolis	2
5 June	Milwaukee	9
12 June	Detroit	7
26 June	Portland	6
10 July	Cleveland	4
17 July	Toronto	9
31 July	Michigan	DNF
14 Aug	Mid Ohio	9
21 Aug	New Hampshire	DNS
4 Sept	Vancouver	DNF
11 Sept	Elkhart Lake	1
18 Sept	Nazareth	7
9 Oct	Laguna Seca	3

Championship: Al Unser Jr. 225, E Fittipaldi 178, P Tracy 152 (Villeneuve 94, sixth).

1995 IndyCar Championship (Reynard-Cosworth)

5 Mar	Miami	1
19 Mar	Surfers' Paradise	DNF
2 Apr	Phoenix	5
9 Apr	Long Beach	DNF
23 Apr	Nazareth	2
28 May	Indianapolis	1
4 June	Milwaukee	6
11 June	Detroit	9
25 June	Portland	P/DNF
9 July	Elkhart Lake	P/1

16 July	Toronto	P/3
23 July	Cleveland	1
30 July	Michigan	10
13 Aug	Mid Ohio	P/3
20 Aug	New Hampshire	4
3 Sept	Vancouver	P/12
10 Sept	Laguna Seca	P/11

Championship: Villeneuve 172, Unser Jr. 161, B Rahal 128.

(Unser's win at Portland was disqualified but reinstated after the end of the season.)